Heritage

A B O V E

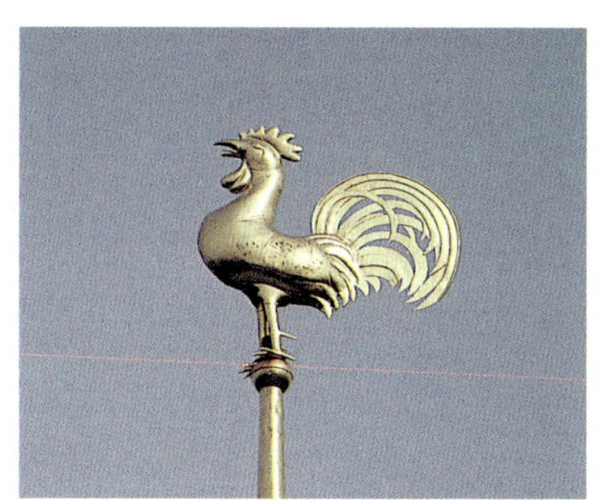

A Tribute TO *Maine's Tradition* OF *Weather Vanes*

Heritage

A B O V E

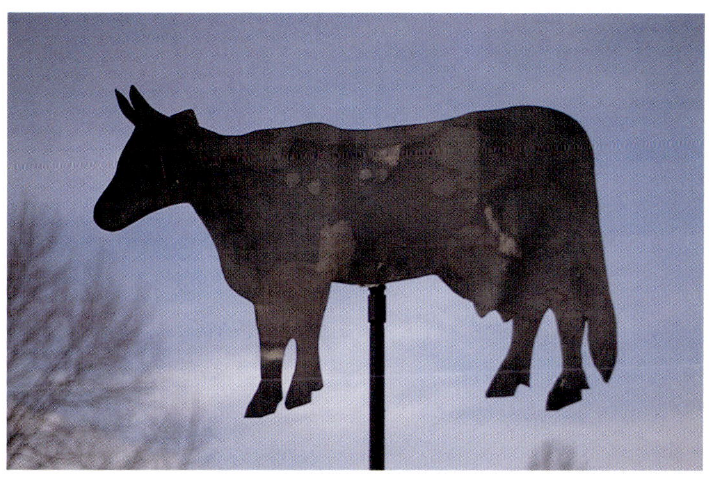

PHOTOGRAPHS & TEXT BY

Marcia Burnell

Down East Books

ISBN 0-89272-278-9

Book design by Edith Allard
Color separations, printing, and binding done in
Hong Kong through Four Colour Imports

5 4 3 2 1

Down East Books, Camden, Maine

Contents

Acknowledgments vi
Introduction vii

Creatures Wild and Tame 1
Ships and the Sea 32
Myth and Symbol 46
Scrolls and Banners 52
Human Endeavors 72

Bibliography 83
Museums Displaying Weather Vanes 84

Acknowledgments

I would like to thank my husband, Gary; daughters Kathy and Kristen; parents Judy and Bob White; and my sister, Linda Coldwell, for their unending support and enthusiasm. At various times they have shared in the adventure of looking for unique weather vanes. I would also like to thank the following individuals and organizations for their generous assistance: Earle G. Shettleworth, Jr., Director of the Maine Historic Preservation Commission; Sam Pennington, Editor of *Maine Antique Digest;* Kenneth and Ida Manko; Peg Pingree; Henry Knoll; the Pejepscot Historical Society, and the Bridgton Historical Society. I am deeply grateful to the people, too numerous to mention, who either allowed me to photograph their vanes or who supplied information on weather vanes.

Introduction

As one travels the towns and back roads of Maine, it is impossible to ignore the abundance and variety of weather vanes still gracing many rooftops. There is a compelling power to these detached, untouchable objects that speaks to one's spirit. A universal reaction of pleasure accompanies the simple sight of a lovely weather vane on high. Whether it is due to the lofty, honored position they occupy or the story behind the form, the fact is, everyone responds to weather vanes.

This book takes a look at Maine's history and character revealed through her weather vanes. The tradition of vanes came with the early settlers from England and has thrived through three centuries of development and change. Maine produced the most famous American weather vane maker. Deacon Shem Drowne (1683–1774) was born in Kittery, moved with his family to Boston in 1692, and later became one of the city's foremost metalsmiths. His work was of such quality that it became a model for future vane makers.

Weather vanes have always been products of both artists and amateurs, reflecting the lifestyles and resources of each. A congenial blend of fine art and folk art evolved that decorated both countryside and city. The poor as well as the rich displayed weather vanes.

The sea god Triton was the subject of the first known weather vane, which dates from 48 B.C. It sat atop the Tower of the Winds in Athens, Greece. Villa owners in pre-Christian Rome also flew weather vanes depicting their gods. However, the forerunner of the New England weather vane appeared in Europe during the Middle Ages and Renaissance, as finials decorating the buildings. Most common were gilded spheres. Crosses were usually placed atop spheres of churches. Nobility in Medieval England put flags and banners on buildings for identification. The English Christian churches commonly used crosses, stars, or cocks for their finials. Of these, only the full-bodied cock fought the wind, so out of necessity it was designed to turn. Since it responded to the wind, it came to be called a weathercock, and for centuries "weathercock" was the generic term for all vanes.

The early English settlers to the New World brought with them the tradition of "fanes," as they called their flags and weather vanes. America's weather vane custom was well established by 1673. However, the weathercocks did not appear in New England until the eighteenth century, for reasons explained later.

The popular weather vane of the early 1700s was the flag or banner. In the New World, where nobility and the class system did not exist, settlers enjoyed flying their own banner, a privilege that was denied them in England, for this gave them a feeling of status and equality. These early vanes had no cardinals (pointers for wind direction) and turned away from the wind. Brass and iron were expensive, so were used sparingly, but because of their enduring qualities a few of these metal vanes still exist. In keeping with a British tradition, vanes were often put on new buildings to show the date of completion. However, some of the oldest have no dates.

Subsistence in eighteenth-century Maine depended heavily on fishing. Codfish, in particular, were the heart of survival for New England coastal towns. Shipbuilders, sailors, lumbermen, and other related tradesmen were all needed to support fishing. These essential trades were common weather vane subjects of the time. Fish proved the ideal shape for weather vanes, as they could glide through the air as easily as through the sea. They were also appealing as a Christian religious symbol. Cardinals were added to vanes in the mid 1700s, and these vanes, unlike the earlier banners, turned into the wind.

The Puritan design for vanes was simple and unadorned. The harsh and austere meeting house with a lovely plain weather vane on top must have made a commanding sight in the center of town. It is believed that the absence of weathercocks in the seventeenth century is due to the Puritan disapproval of graven images. The cock has long been associated with papal and episcopal churches. Weathercocks of that period only existed outside of Puritan New England. However, in the eighteenth century, meeting houses and churches customarily used either cockerel or swallow-tailed vanes.

In 1782, the bald eagle was designated the official symbol for the newly independent nation, and eagle weather vanes popped up everywhere. The early ones were slightly built and somewhat weak in appearance. Not until the Civil War years did they come to convey strength and power. Another weather vane theme used to symbolize America was the Indian. Wildlife also provided subjects; anything from wolves, bears, and wild turkeys to rattlesnakes and moose was perched on barns and houses.

All vanes of the eighteenth and early nineteenth centuries were handcrafted. There were two distinct types, silhouette and three-dimensional, made from either wood or metal. Most fragile of all were the silhouette wooden vanes, for when water soaked into the pores and froze, it caused the wood to split. Most vanes of the period were painted wood and were vulnerable to weather and fire, so very few vanes from this period have survived.

Nineteenth-century New England enjoyed the prosperity brought by merchant and whaling ships. Clipper ships, the fastest sailing vessels yet designed, briefly dominated the shipping world between 1840 and 1850. With their sharp bow, deep stern, slender and low-slung hull, and lofty masts carrying massive sails, they could transport goods faster than any other ship in the world. Tea from China was the most important cargo, though the gold fields of California and Australia also created vital markets.

The shipbuilders were prosperous, and seaport communities benefitted from the merchant trade. It was only natural that clipper ship weather vanes were commonly seen at that time, for they symbolized people's interests and investments.

The imagery was particularly appropriate since both sailing ships and weather vanes respond to the wind. The early clipper vanes were carved from wood, some three-dimensional, others flat. Many were made by the sea captains and sailors themselves to help pass the long idle hours at sea. The rigging and sails, often of copper or cloth, were held by fragile masts. Few of these original wooden works of art have survived, but copies in iron and copper are relatively abundant. Some are quite elaborate.

The clippers also brought a foreign influence to New England, which was reflected in designs used on weather vanes. Chinese dragons became a fashionable subject, and their long, slender shape was quite effective in the wind.

The whaling industry also flourished during the nineteenth century. Whale products were crucial to the everyday life of the New Englander: oil for lamps, baleen ("whalebone") for many and varied uses, and spermaceti for candles made whaling centers wealthy. Like their brethren on the clipper ships, whaling captains and crew were apt to carve weather vanes. They made ships, whales, whalemen blowing their horns, and other whaling symbols. Anything related to the whaling industry was perched on buildings. The sperm whale was popular even though its profile—heavy in front, tapering to a narrow tail—was the antithesis of what a weather vane shape should be.

Fish vanes were still much used, although new varieties became more prominent than the cod that had been popular in the 1700s. Mackerel fishing, for example, became important in the early 1800s. Since mackerel are food for swordfish, the sighting of swordfish meant good fishing, and both of these fish were models for vanes. As time went on, swordfish became the ultimate game fish. This established a booming tourist economy for New England by the early 1900s, and the sleek, graceful shape of the swordfish then topped many a building.

Other popular early nineteenth-century weather vane subjects were "Liberty caps," the angel Gabriel, and scrolls (including lyres). Scrolls and lyres seem to have been used most often. The scroll vanes were an extension of the earlier banner designs. They enhanced the basic old style with the delicate detailed lines of classical themes. The lyre became the dominant classical motif for scrolls of the period. Scrolls were the most common design for the vanes on New England churches. (The same holds true today.) They were designed for the classical revival churches that epitomize New England. The lyre, because it signifies song, makes a fitting church weather vane.

Three basic elements make up the scroll design: an arrow at the front, a scroll or lyre shape for the body, and a tail decorated with stars, sunbursts, tulips, etc. Being flat, scrolls were simple to build and easy to transport.

The mid 1800s saw a revival of medieval-style flags and banners. They were larger than the simple Puritan "fanes" of a century before, and came to be mass produced as the Industrial Revolution gathered momentum. Usually they were made of copper, whereas the earlier ones had been made of iron. The scrolls also became more intricate.

Farmers seemed to be natural whittlers, turning out highly individual and stylized weather vanes. A simple arrow, paired with an animal silhouette, was an ideal and commonly used motif. Farm animals of all shapes and sizes graced the barns. Most popular of all was the chicken, but sheep, pigs, ducks, horses, cows, and other farm animals all had places of distinction atop barns. They were painted in realistic colors and usually flew without cardinals, since farmers already knew the wind so well. They were placed on barns for grandeur and beauty more than as wind indicators.

Gamecock images also sat on barns, as did farming tools, such as plows. However, due to the Industrial Revolution, only a minority of farmers continued to carve their one-of-a-kind wooden weather vanes by the mid-nineteenth century. The unique wooden forms began to disappear.

James Lombard, of the Bridgton area, is Maine's most honored weather vane maker. During the 1880s, his skillfully carved wooden vanes, set on area farms, won him local recognition. He is best known for his distinctive method of carving fanciful tail feathers on roosters. Today his work is exhibited at both the Shelburne Museum in Vermont and the Smithsonian Institution in Washington, D.C., among others. Few Lombard vanes are still left in Maine.

Mass production allowed people to buy vanes cheaper than they could make them. Cast-iron vanes flourished, with most of them found in Maine. Weather vane catalogs offered something for everyone. Sheep vanes were hung on textile mills, firemen or fire trucks on firehouses. There were images of country doctors, steamboats, oxen, trains, shuttles for weavers, anvils, the arm and hammer, and various other symbols of business. Carriage houses frequently boasted a sporting theme, with dogs, geese, deer, fox or a sleek horse sitting atop the roofs. Mythological figures such as Greek gods, mermaids, Pegasus, and Triton (half man, half fish) were popular.

Farms in the nineteenth century displayed two different styles of horse vanes. The powerful work horses were appropriately cast in iron, while the lighter sporting horses, such as trotters and hunters, were commonly made of sheet coper. Even the sheet copper vanes frequently had heads or other body parts in iron, zinc, bronze, or lead, which allowed greater detail while giving balance to the vane. (This method of combining different materials on one vane was also used for other vane forms besides horses.)

Weather vanes were so well liked that frequently they stood on every building a family owned, even the outbuilding. The bigger the building, the bigger the weather vane.

Sheet copper vanes came into favor in the late nineteenth century, and cast-iron vanes became less common. Copper was durable and relatively easy to work. It was also lightweight, making it relatively easy to carry and mount the vanes. Also, the smooth edge held gold leaf for a half century, much longer than did wood, zinc, or iron. This was an important factor, as gilded vanes were the fashion at that time. Copper vanes were not allowed to acquire a blue-green patina. This was also a period of grace and intricacy. Copper flowers and glass feathers abounded on weather vanes. Peacocks and swans were frequently seen on rooftops from the late 1800s to the early 1900s. Church vanes were golden.

Vanes made after World War II were mainly of the silhouette type. They were either stamped out of flat metal and painted, or they were slightly molded cast aluminum and invariably painted black. They seem unimaginative when compared to the unique and carefully crafted weather vanes of earlier times. For the most part, today's vanes are lesser copies of that proud past.

But there are a few exceptions. Even in today's fast-paced, mass-produced world there are still individuals who desire a unique handcrafted vane, and there are talented artisans who welcome the challenge of creating them. These men and women proudly practice an ancient craft by painstakingly hammering, carving, or molding raw material into a unique form that is a glorious blend of whimsey and function. Weather vanes are works of art that dignify any rooftop.

When we admire a historic Maine weather vane, we are seeing more than just a lovely shape against the sky. The old vanes are powerful symbols of all that was vital to the region's history; a heritage on high representing the pride and endeavor of past generations.

Maine's history, in the form of her weather vanes, is being taken from her. Antique vanes are highly prized as folk art and command high prices at auction and in antique stores.* Unfortunately, most of these old vanes are sold to out-of-state buyers. Maine's historic vanes are now found throughout the country, with the heaviest concentrations in New York and California.

Tragically, the few remaining old vanes are the target of thieves who scale roofs and steeples to strip them off their perches. They know that unscrupulous agents and dealers will pay huge sums of money for authentic old vanes. Some speculate that these greedy thieves have even used helicopters to get at their vanes; others insist that this is just a myth. Whatever methods are used, they are obviously effective, for weather vane thefts have become all too common. In today's world, the owner of an antique weather vane would do well to replace it with a replica on the rooftop. The original can then be safely displayed indoors.

In spite of the fact that so many weather vanes have been sold, legitimately or otherwise, to collectors, there are still mounted old vanes to be seen along Maine's roads. It is not difficult to observe fine nineteenth-century vanes on church steeples. The First Parish Church, in Portland, is topped by what is thought to be the oldest vane (1760) in the state that is still hung on a roof. A drive along back roads will also reveal an occasional vane from the 1800s. Museums, historical societies, and antique stores are great sources for those interested in a closer look. Records of weather vanes can be found in local libraries, town and state historical societies, and in parish records.

In the pages that follow, I have presented a broad selection that best conveys the beauty and individuality of the many wonderful weather vanes that can still be spotted against the Maine sky. The selection process was difficult, for I have photographed many more vanes than it was possible to show, and each had its own character and individual history. The antiquity of one, the artistic quality of another, or the individuality of still another were all taken into account. Unfortunately, due to space restrictions, many fascinating weather vanes could not be included in these pages. However, the outstanding examples shown do offer a good sampling of what

---

* The record price for a weather vane sold at auction was for a large copper and zinc horse and rider, sold at Sotheby's in January 1990 for an astounding $770,000. It was made circa 1860 by J. Howard and Company in West Bridgewater, Massachusetts. The previous record was $203,500 for a locomotive and tender sold in March 1987 in Bolton, Massachusetts. The third highest price was paid for the famous eighteenth-century wooden rooster from Portland, Maine, which sold for $121,000 in July 1986.

is out there to be seen. The historical significance of some stand in contrast to the contemporary design of others. No other art symbol is so effective in revealing the lifestyles and interests of those below. A pleasing blend of past and present is there for all to enjoy.

A Note to the Reader:

Much of Maine's history is well documented; however, for some weather vanes little or nothing has been recorded. In many cases the details passed on with the original owners. Where possible, I have accumulated stories and facts, but for some vanes I have had to speculate on the history.

No owners' names or locations of privately owned vanes are given in this book.

—M.B.

Facing page: *A late-nineteenth-century vane shows Smuggler, a famous trotter. It has a wonderful patina highlighted by unoxidized copper. Every line of this beautifully stylized figure expresses speed and spirit.*

Creatures Wild and Tame

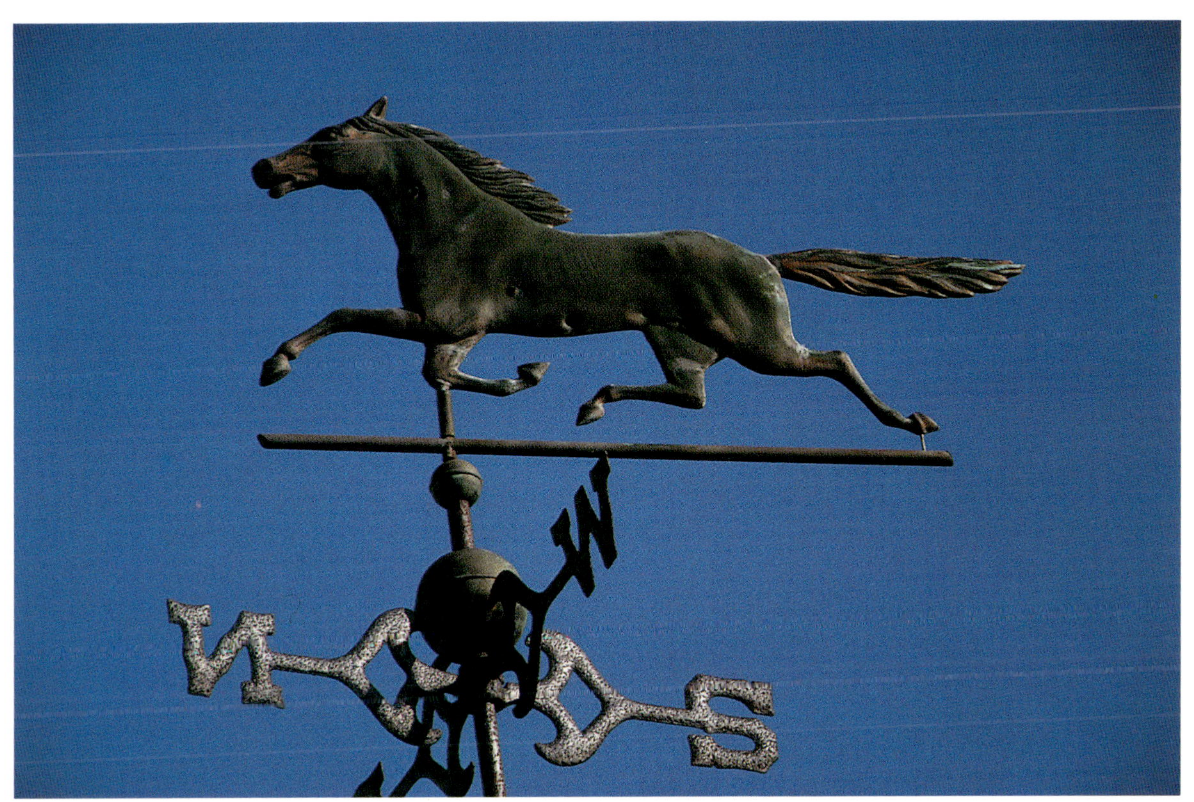

The weathered wooden cupola of days gone by sets off this copper horse vane. It is another likeness of Smuggler, and was made between 1870 and 1900.

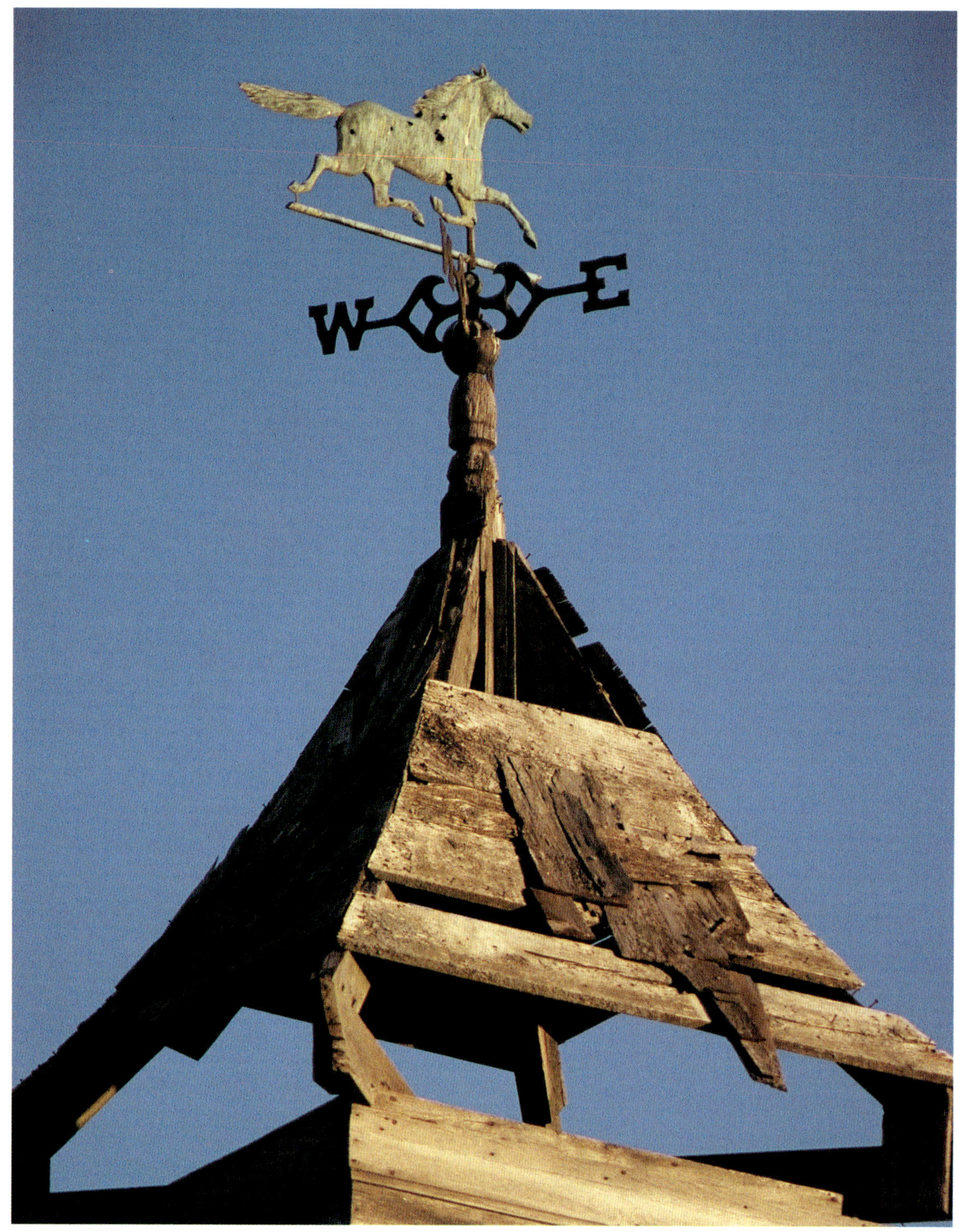

Early fall foliage provides a pleasing backdrop for a handsome hackney dated between 1860 and 1880. The gold leaf is wearing off, leaving behind a nice verdigris patina. This copper animal came from the Livermore Falls area. Courtesy of Kenneth and Ida Manko

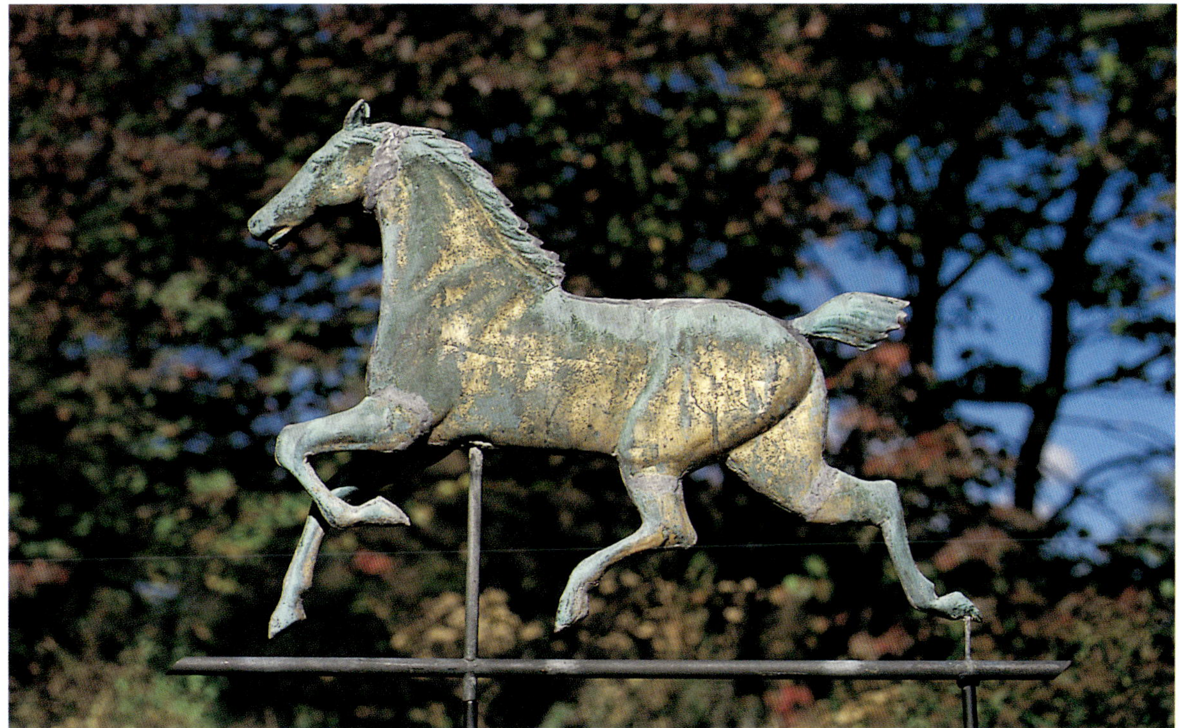

Standing guard on an old barn is this spirited silhouette horse (or perhaps pony) from the 1880s. Weather has damaged the cardinals and rusted out the post so it can no longer turn in the wind.

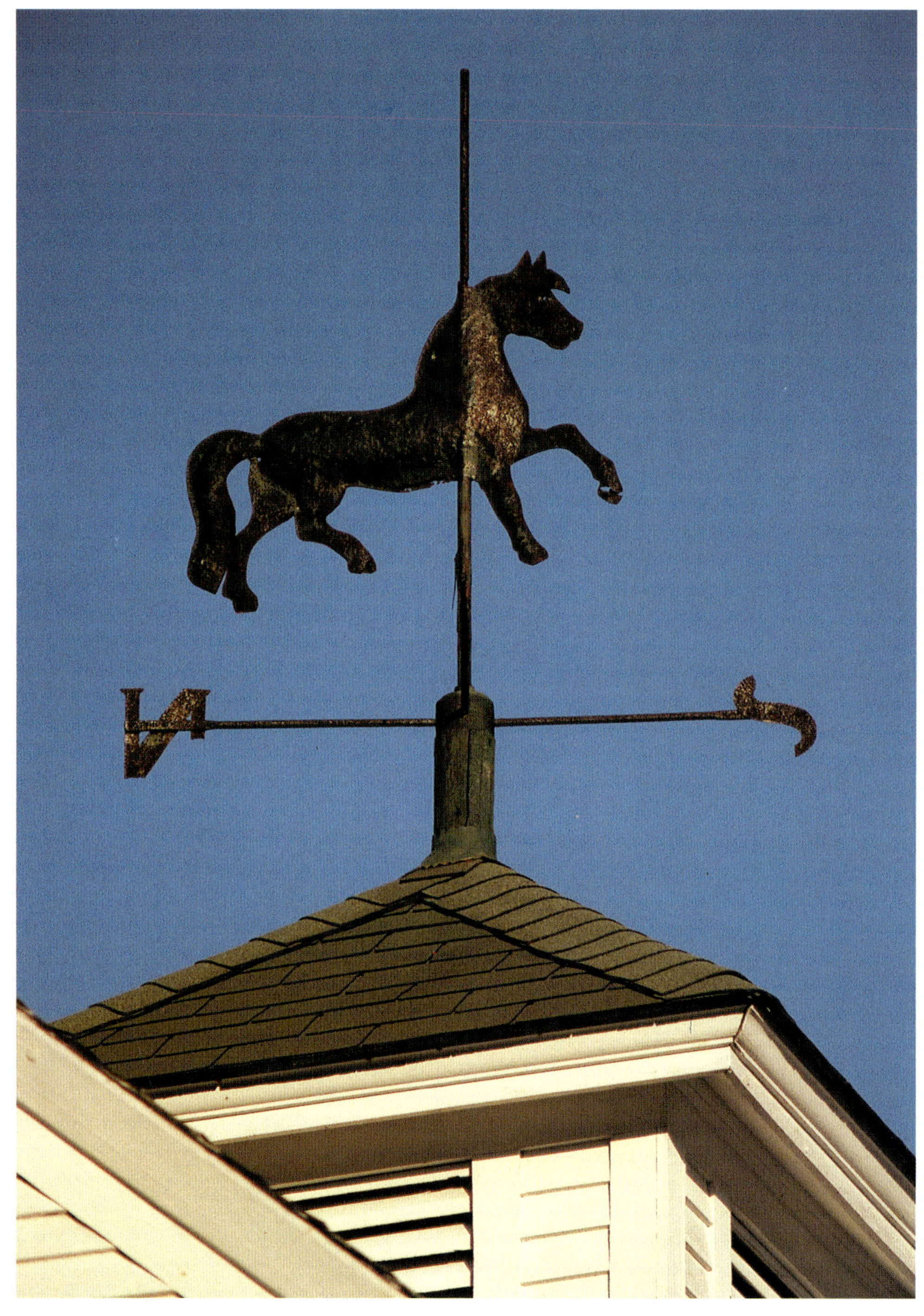

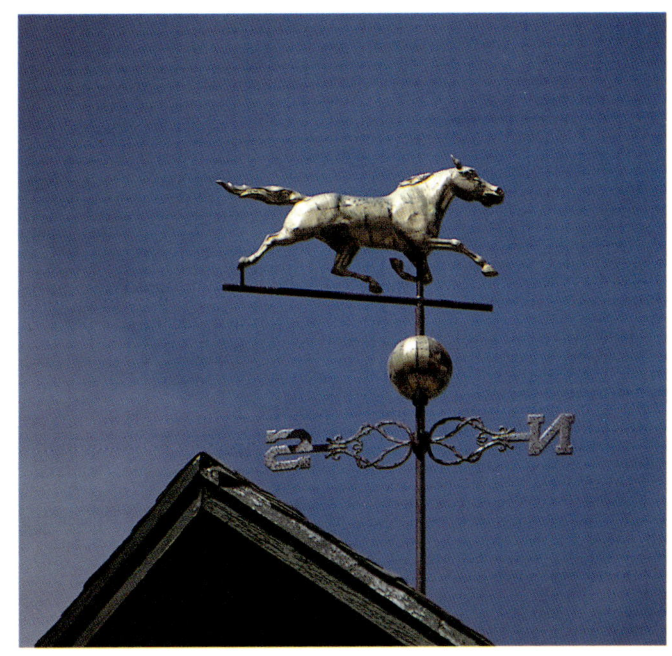

This well-formed running horse dates back to the 1880s. It is covered with gold leaf and sits above an attractive gilded ball. Its sturdy muscularity provides an interesting contrast to the elegantly streamlined form of the horse vane on page 1.

This remarkable gold-leaf–covered Black Hawk has been in the same family since it was first mounted in 1876. The present owner grew up with it on his parents' estate and has moved it himself to three different homes. The vane beautifully portrays the spirit of this famous Morgan horse, and the dents—and even bullet marks—it has accumulated over the decades only add interest to the surface.

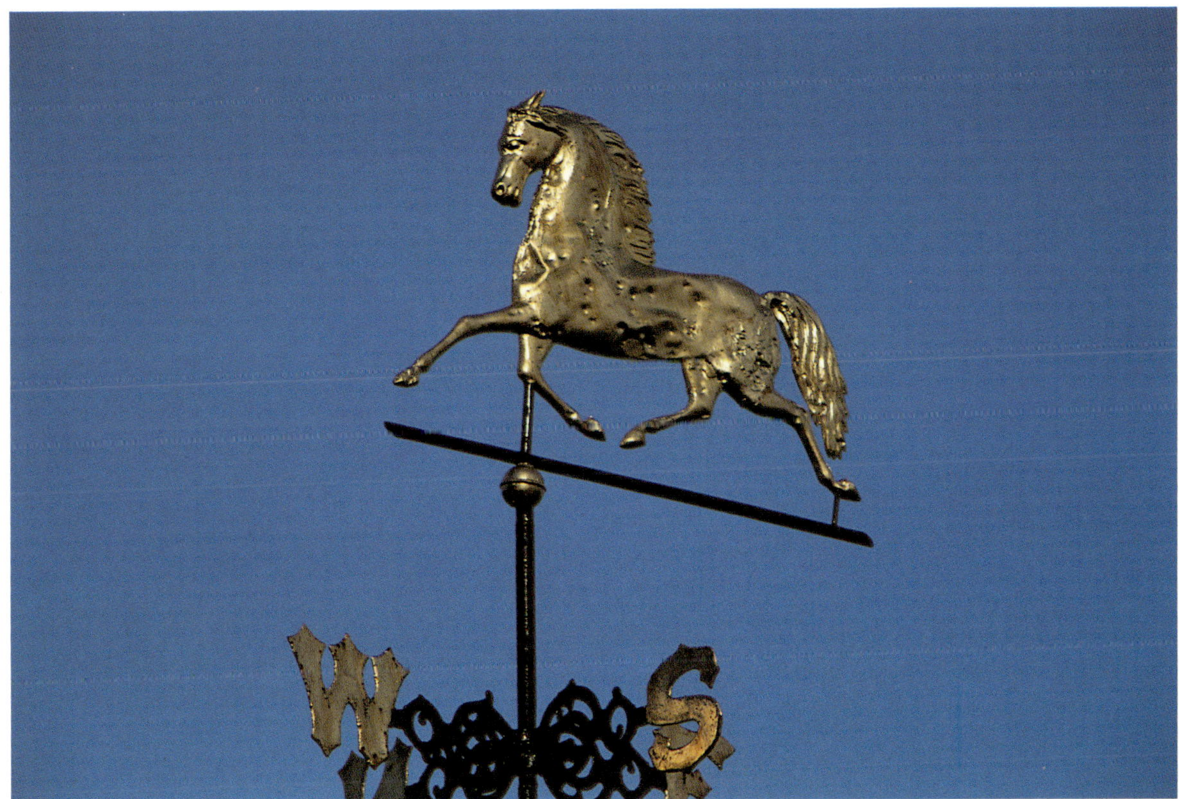

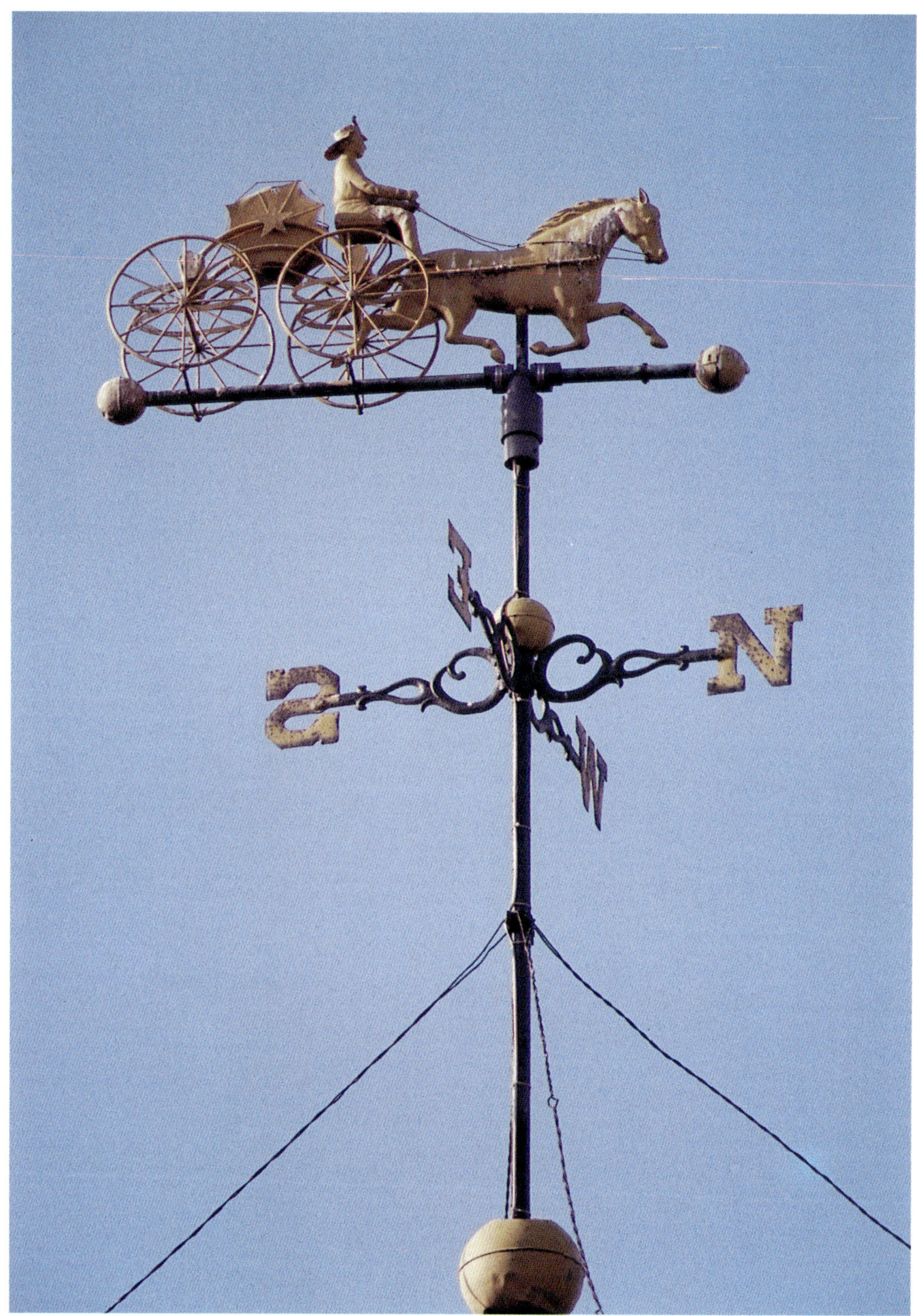
N
S

Facing page: *The famous late-nineteeth-century hosecart vane on the Hallowell fire station was stolen on the stormy night of November 15, 1983. It was too well known for the thieves to be able to sell it on the antiques market. Two days after the theft, a man contacted Sam Pennington, editor of the* Maine Antique Digest, *to begin negotiations that would lead to the vane's recovery one week after it was stolen. Pennington met the would-be fence in New Hampshire, and they drove down one dark country road after another until they met up with a second man who handed over the weather vane in exchange for one thousand dollars in ransom from the insurance company.*

The vane was rehung, this time hooked up to an alarm system. The person who contacted Pennington was later apprehended, but jumped bail and was never brought to trial. As for Mr. Pennington, he says, "Never again."

The antique hosecart vane is fifty-three inches long and is painted old yellow.

The copper trotting horse with sulky looks as if it is having an early-morning workout. The age of this piece is unknown, but it appears to be from the early to mid twentieth century.

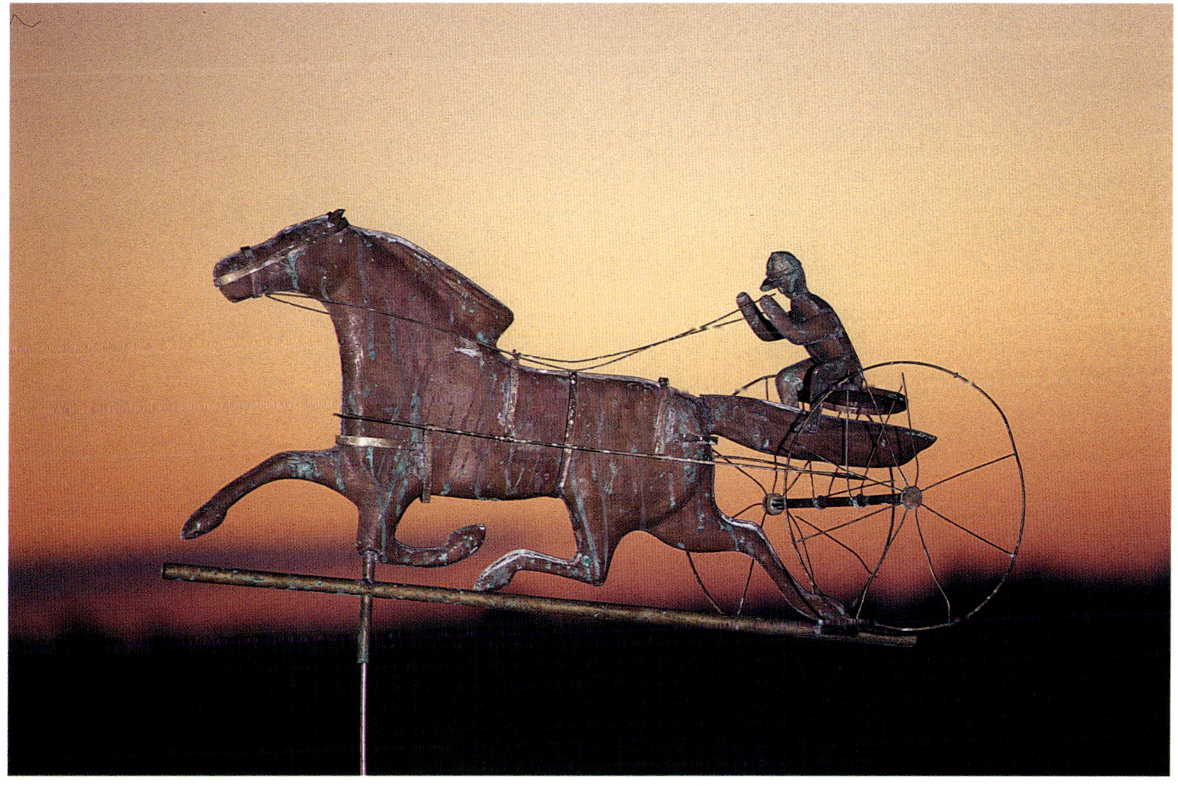

This free-spirited vane shows a stagecoach and six horses. The details add so much to the mood of this cut-out work: the different postures of the passengers, two of whom hold parasols, convey a sense of motion and humor; the dog brings a sense of fun and frolic. The vane probably dates from the 1940s, and appears to be made from painted sheet metal.

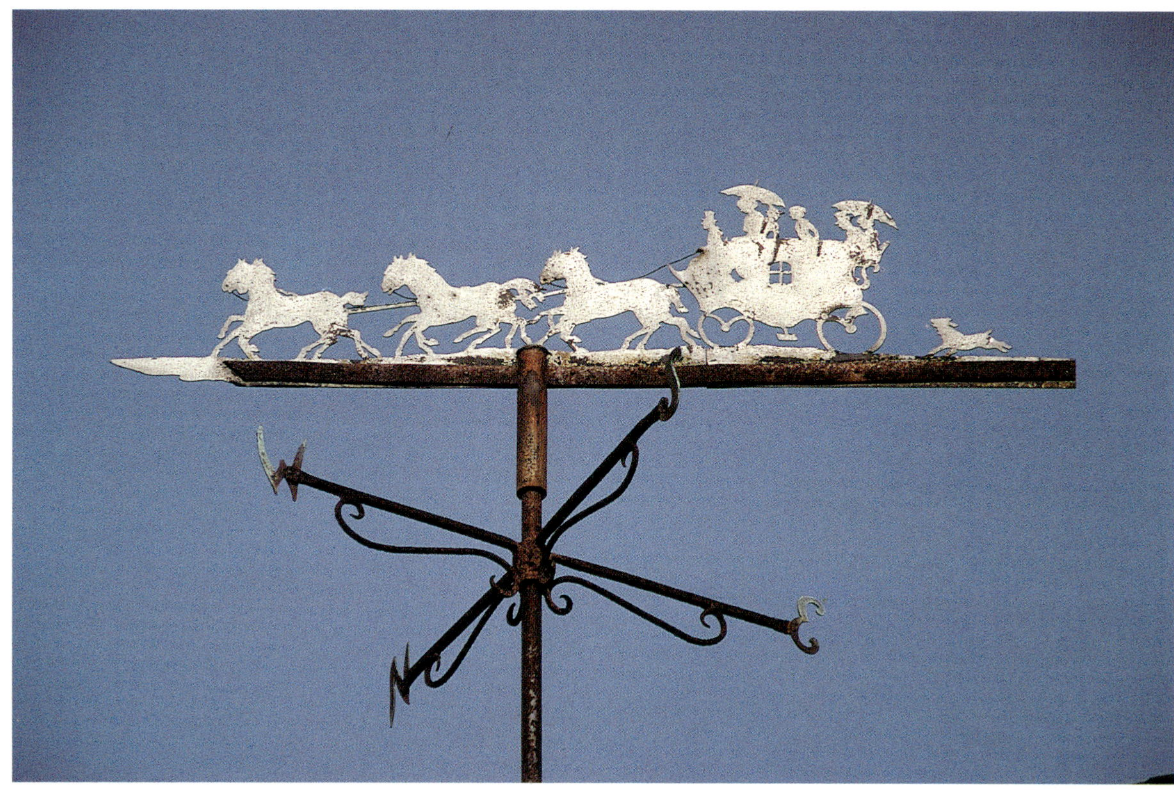

This copper pig is engaged in an uphill battle, probably due to high winds. It has a well shaped, accurate design and a definite personality. Age unknown.

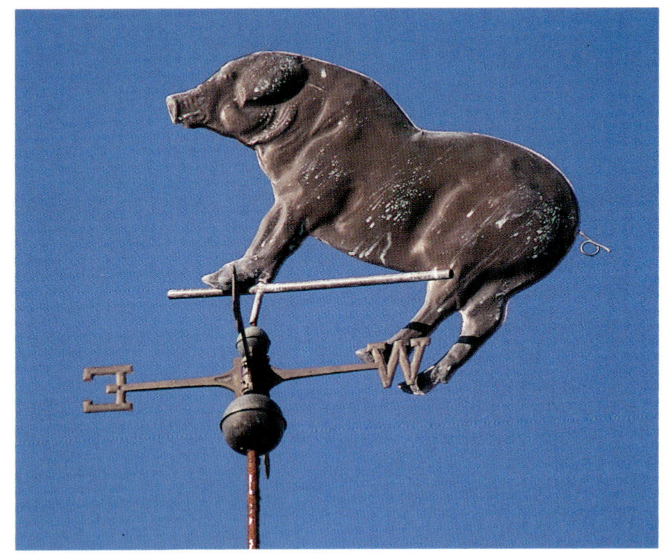

A proud copper pig with its nose in the air makes it easy to see why these animals are favorite weather vane subjects. The alert positioning of the ears, the jaunty attitude of the head, and the distinct corkscrew tail combine with the pitted surface to add interest. This is a newer vane, probably dating from the 1960s.

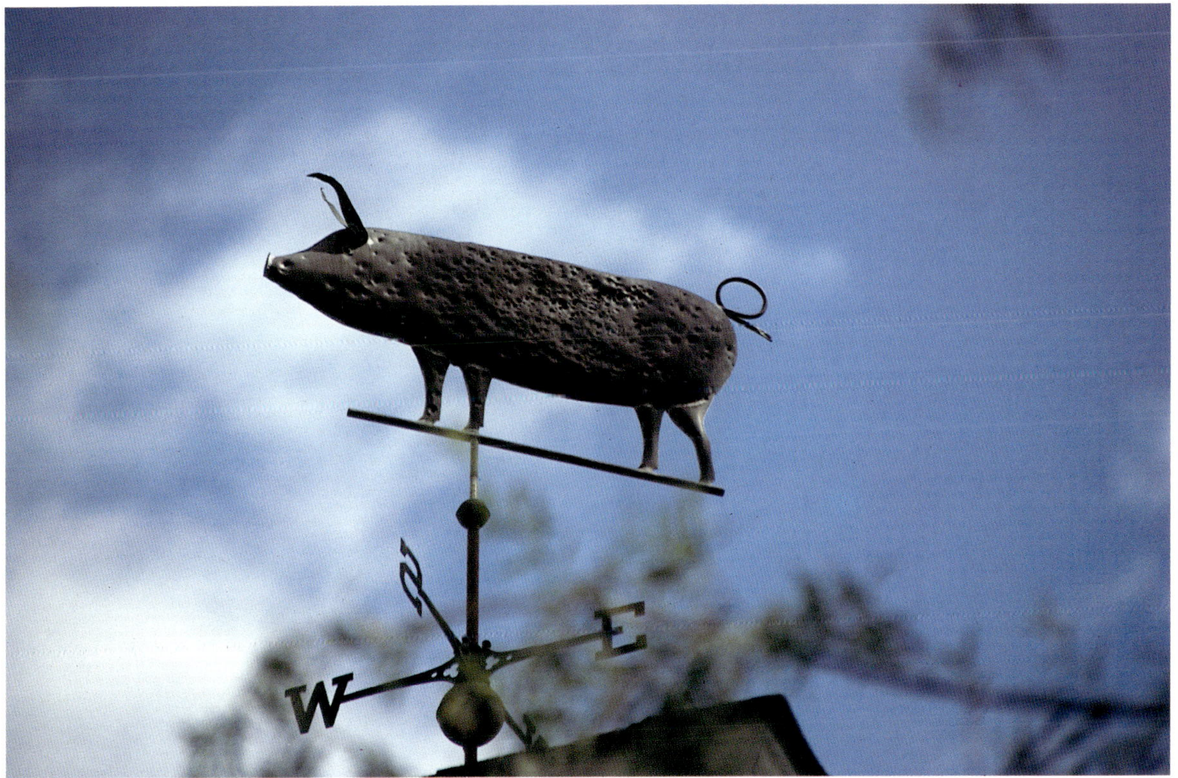

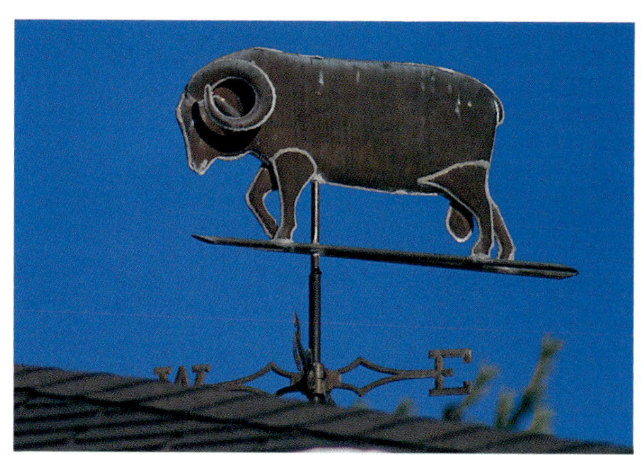

Blacksmiths historically have made a large number of weather vanes. More recently though, the trend has been toward other craftsmen. This hammered copper ram is a good example of the artistry of Barry Norling, a sculptor from Skowhegan. He is known for his emphasis on form rather than detail. Bold, clean lines make his objects easily recognizable from the ground. The vane stands above the barn of another popular Maine artist.

This 1880s rooster is a true heritage of Maine, carved by the state's most honored vane maker, James Lombard. Its distinctive tail feathers are representative of Lombard's style. This particular rooster was discovered in a barn a few years ago. It had been blown down and broken during a windstorm but has since been repaired. At some point a second coat of paint was applied, but traces of red and yellow from the first coat can be seen.
Courtesy of the Bridgton Historical Society

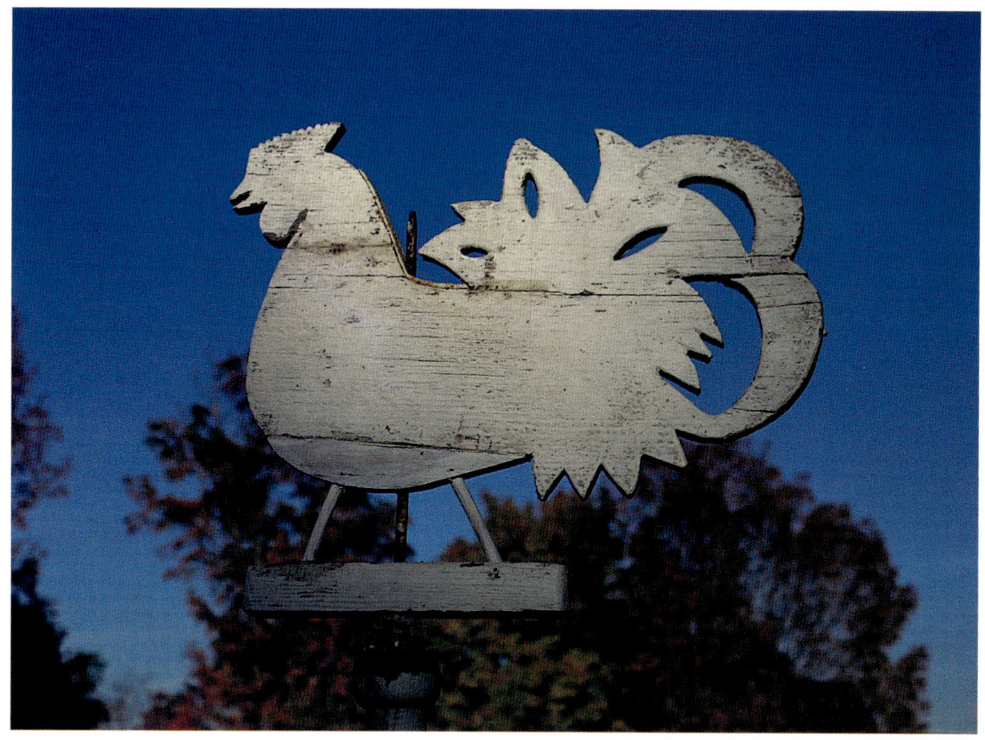

Famous Maine poet Robert Peter Tristram Coffin (1892–1955) designed the fanciful rooster with the bold flowing lines. Did he have this vane in mind when he penned the following poem?

THE WEATHER VANE

A man should choose with careful eye
The things to be remembered by.

When I was knee-high to a man,
My father hired Tom McCann.

Tom's days were beanrows without end
And rotting shingles still to mend.

But one blue day the man carved out
An arrow clean as a small boy's shout.

He set up near where God may be
His arrow on a tall pine tree.

The years that broke his willing heart
Could never rend this man apart.

The years that snowed upon his hair
Could never harm him anywhere.

I wish that men might think of me
Along with ships far out to sea,

Think of me in terms of weather,
Mix me and thunderheads together,

Remember me by a weather vane
Pointing to beauty and the rain.

(From *Collected Poems of Robert P. Tristram Coffin*, new and enlarged edition. New York: The Macmillan Company, 1948.)

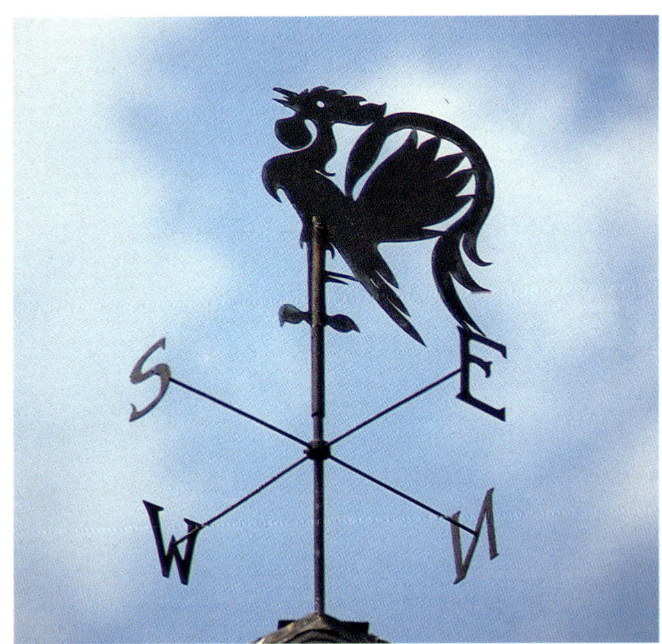

This primitive mid-nineteenth-century wooden rooster is made out of four pieces of wood, with a metal strip forming the wattle. The weathered wood speaks eloquently of decades past. The vane came from a farm in southwestern Maine and was probably whittled by the farmer himself. Farm animals of all shapes and sizes graced the barns, but the most popular of all was the cockerel.

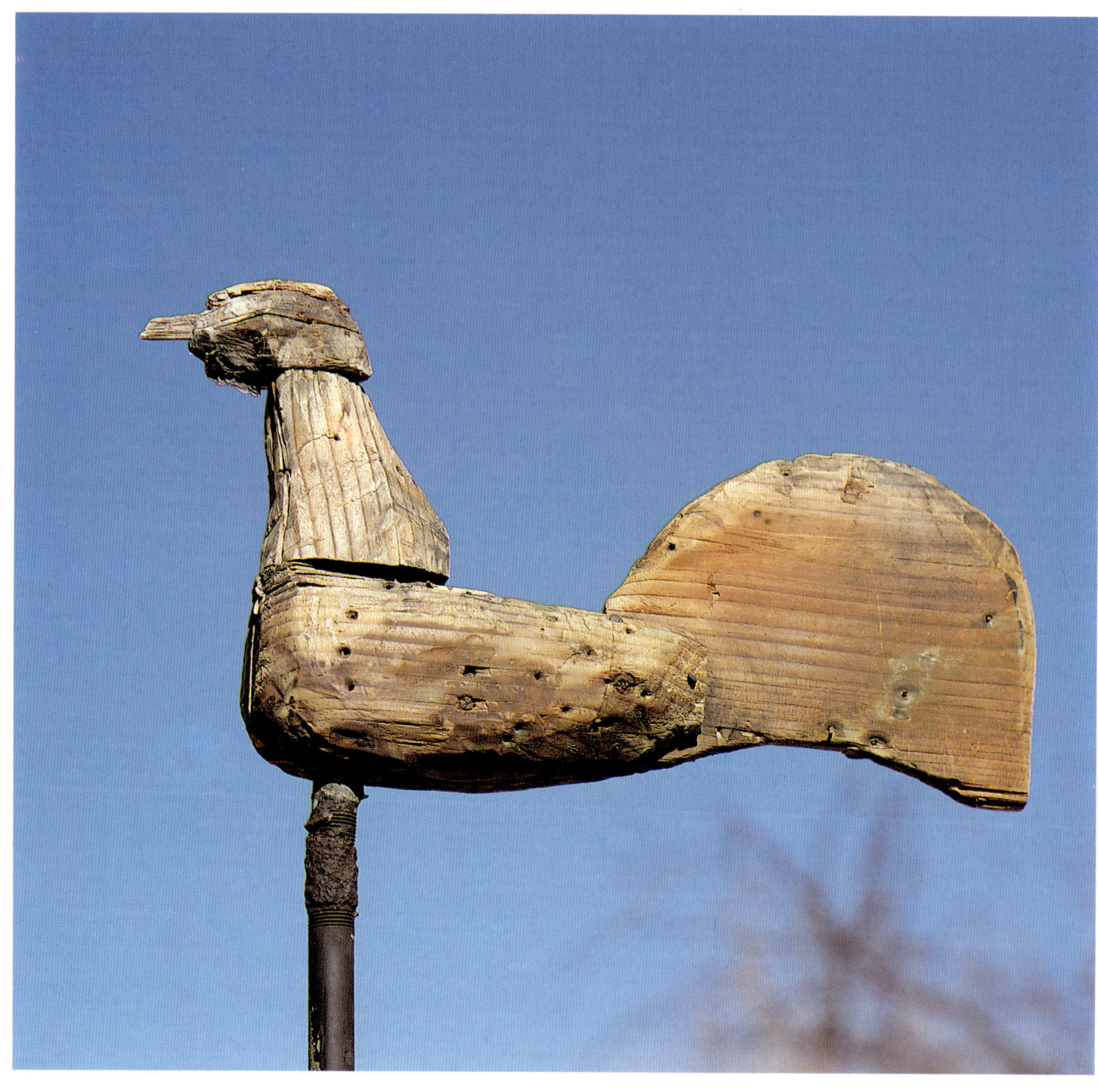

This unique wooden dove of peace made in 1806 has been well preserved. It was carved for the second First Parish Meeting House in Brunswick by Samuel Melcher and was designed by Melcher's wife. The dove is forty-six inches from beak to tail and stands eighteen high. A six-inch tin leaf hangs from the beak. Traces of the original yellow paint or gold leaf are still on the wood. It was taken down in 1845, and has since been held by the Pejepscot Historical Society in Brunswick. Courtesy of the Pejepscot Historical Society

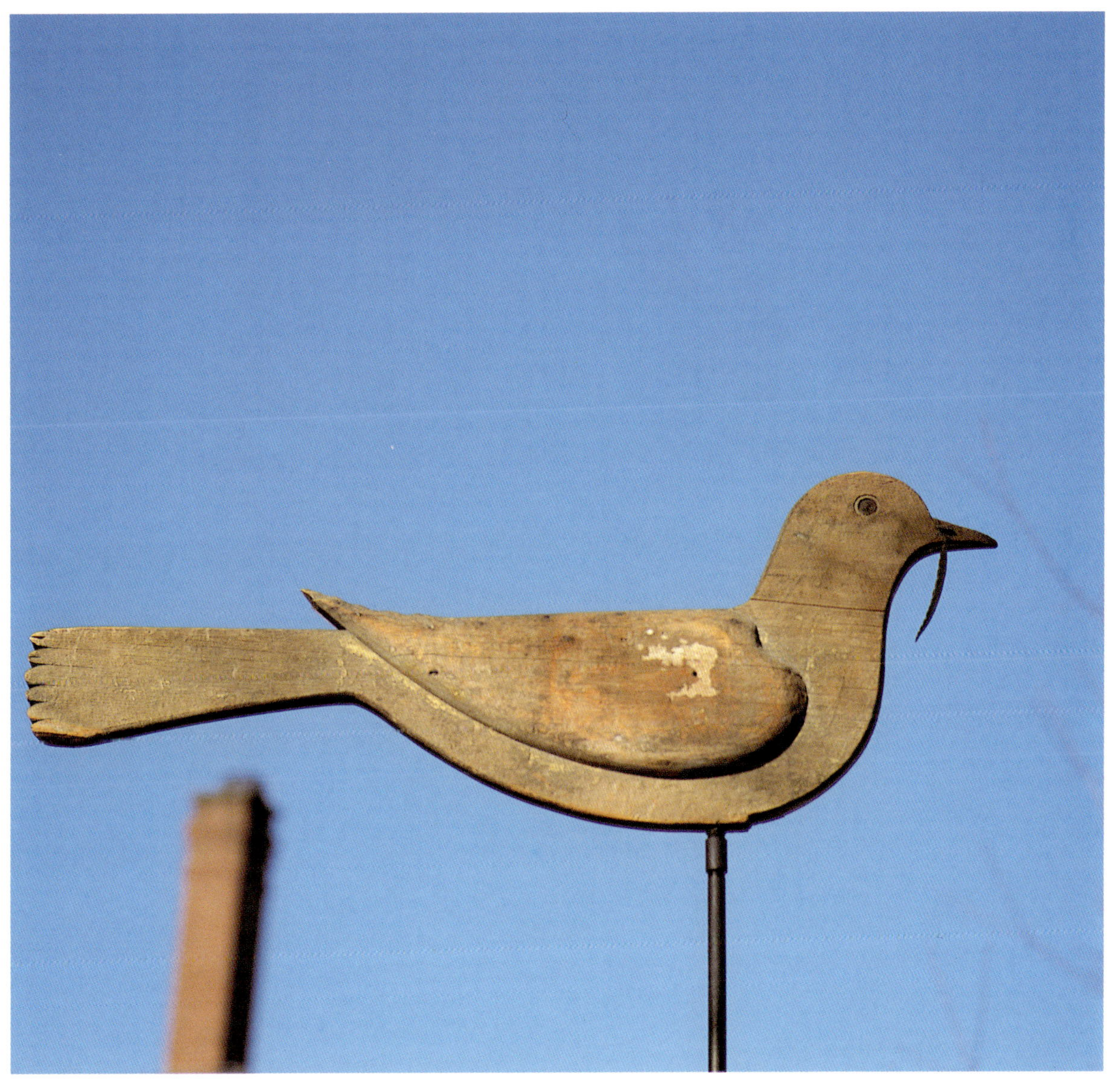

A beautifully stylized crowing rooster rests on the former Brunswick home of author Harriet Beecher Stowe (1811–1896). It is probably a 1930s vane made of iron.

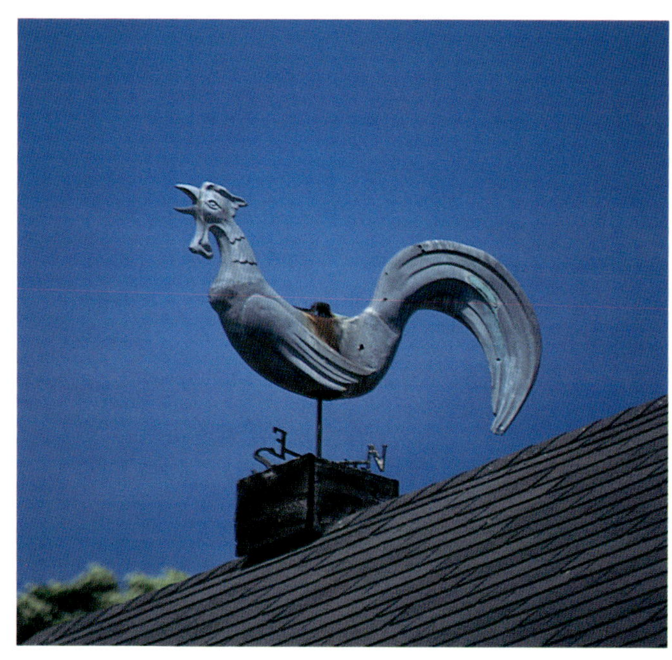

The crowing chanticleer probably is made of iron, judging by the way it has rusted. It appears to be a late 1800s vane and is perched on a large ball surrounded by decorative cardinals.

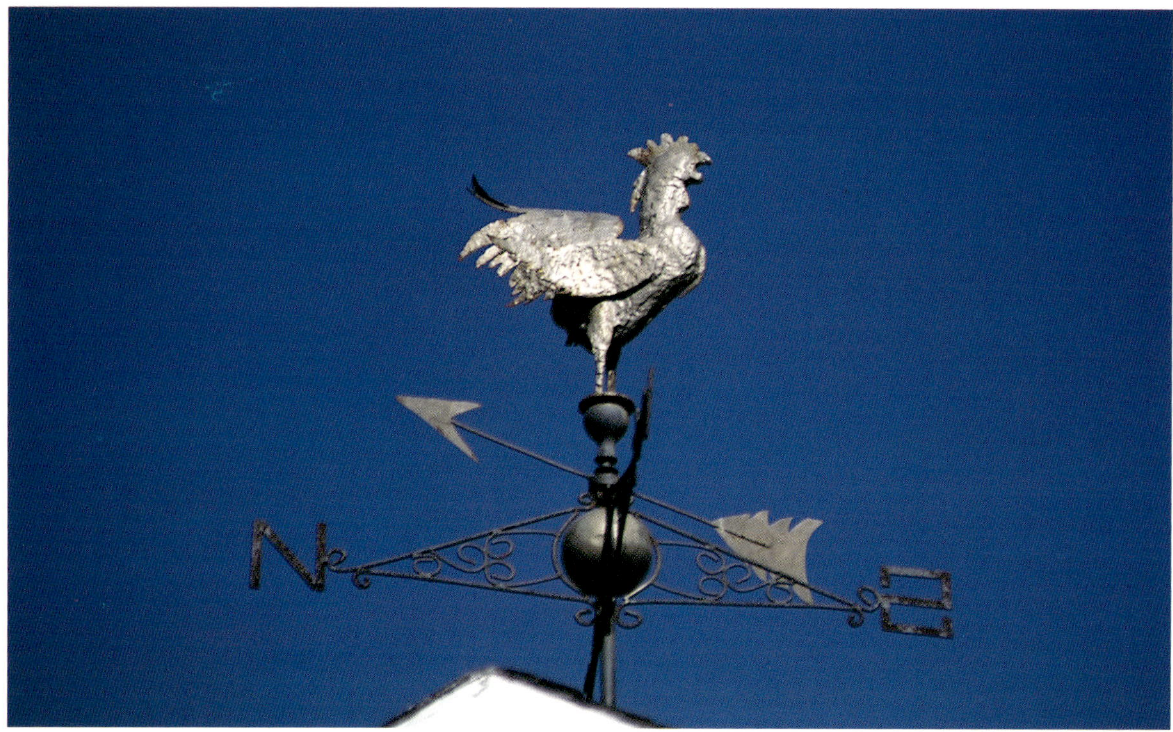

A proud rooster makes a grand topping for this graceful cupola. It appears to date from the 1870s or 1880s.

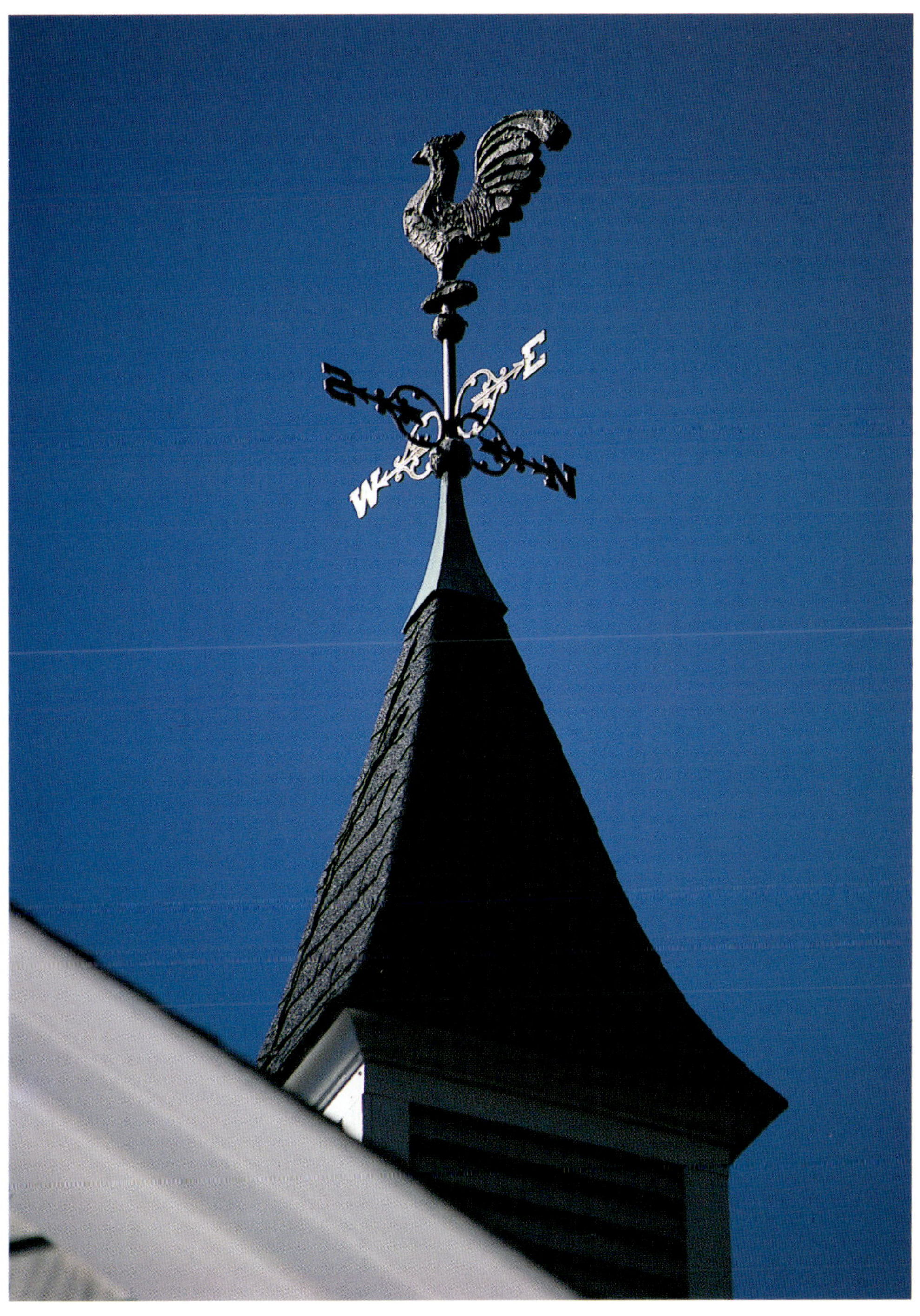

A replica vane now tops St.Mary's of the Virgin in Falmouth. Early photographs indicate that the original rooster was mounted when the Norman tower was added in 1902. In 1986 the vane was stolen, and after extensive research, an exact duplicate was commissioned. Precautions have been taken to prevent another theft.

This proud crowing rooster has a highly stylized tail. The vane is covered with gold leaf.

Because of their association with Christianity, roosters frequently are used as themes for church weather vanes.

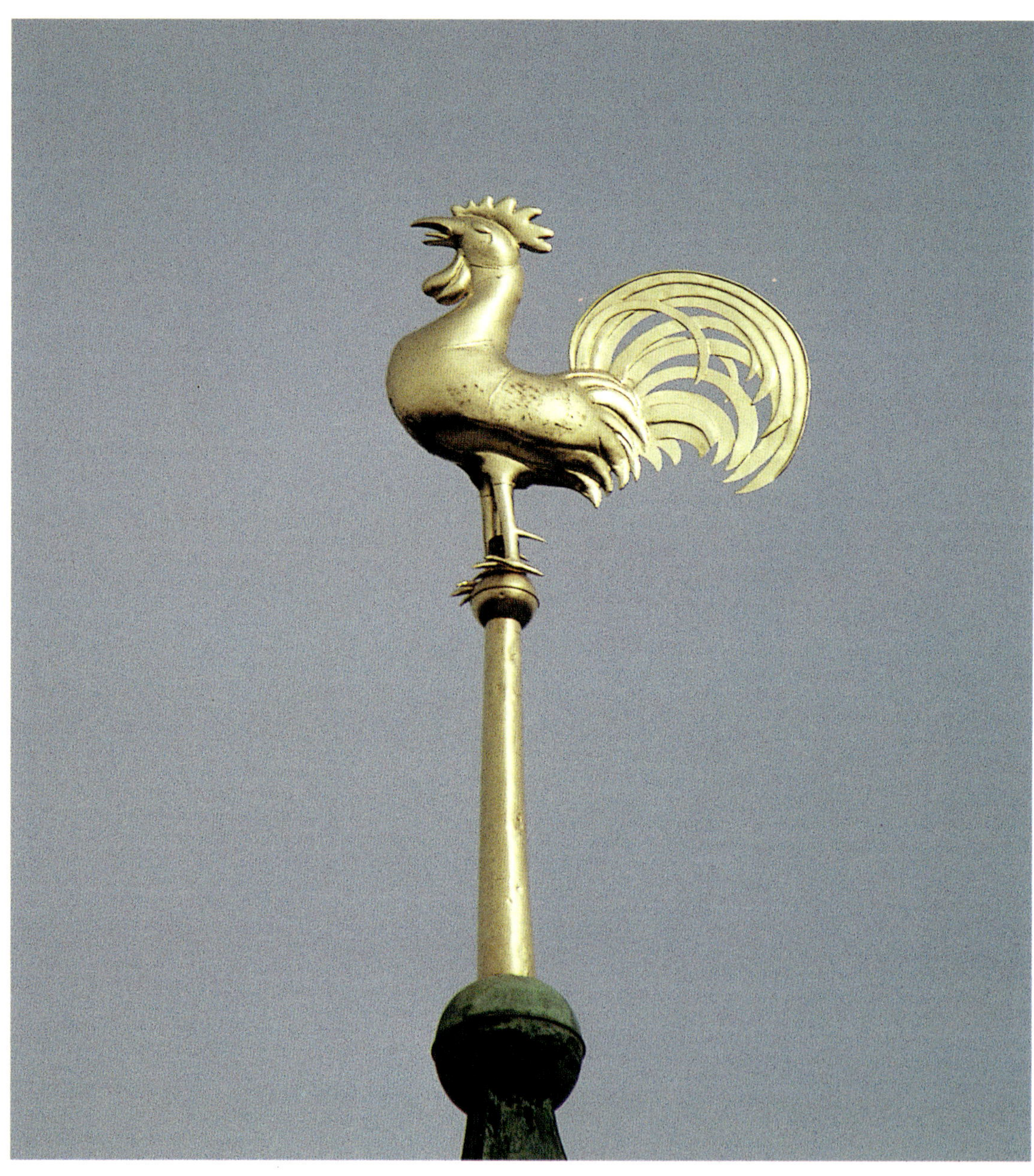

The bald eagle has been a favorite weather vane theme ever since it was designated the national symbol in 1782. This shining example covered with gold leaf graces a bank in Damariscotta that was built in 1979.

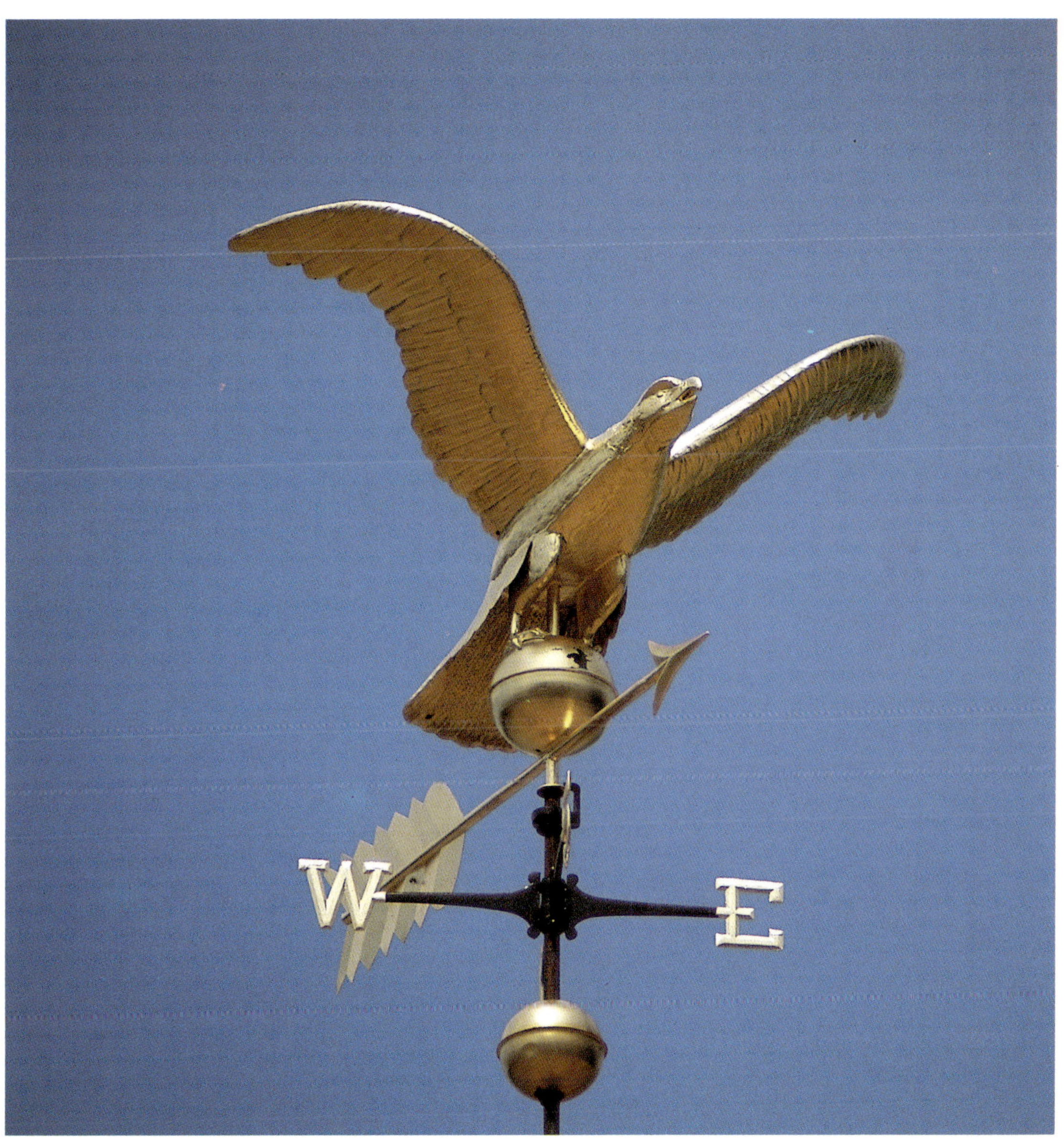

This iron cow is from the early 1800s. It was a first-anniversary gift to the present owners, who wisely keep it indoors, prominently displayed on a living room wall.

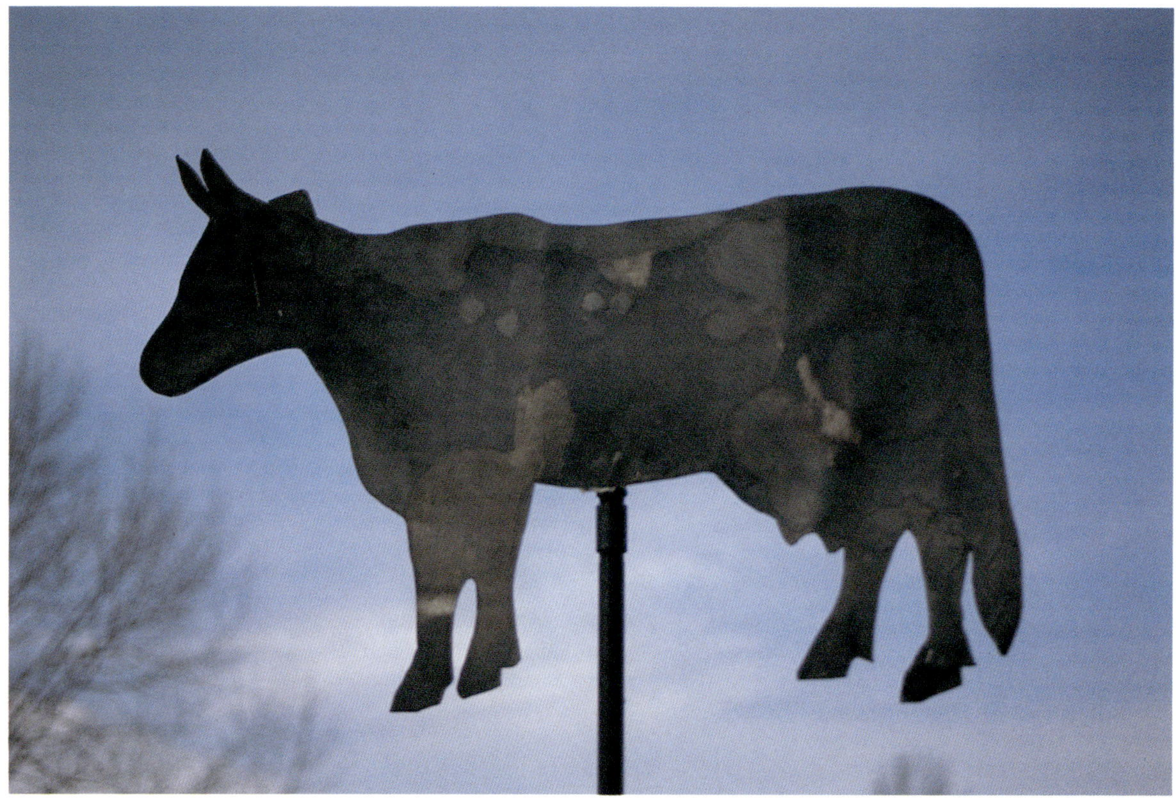

An early 1900s copper cow has aged beautifully over the years. It clearly shows the bullet holes commonly suffered by weather vanes.

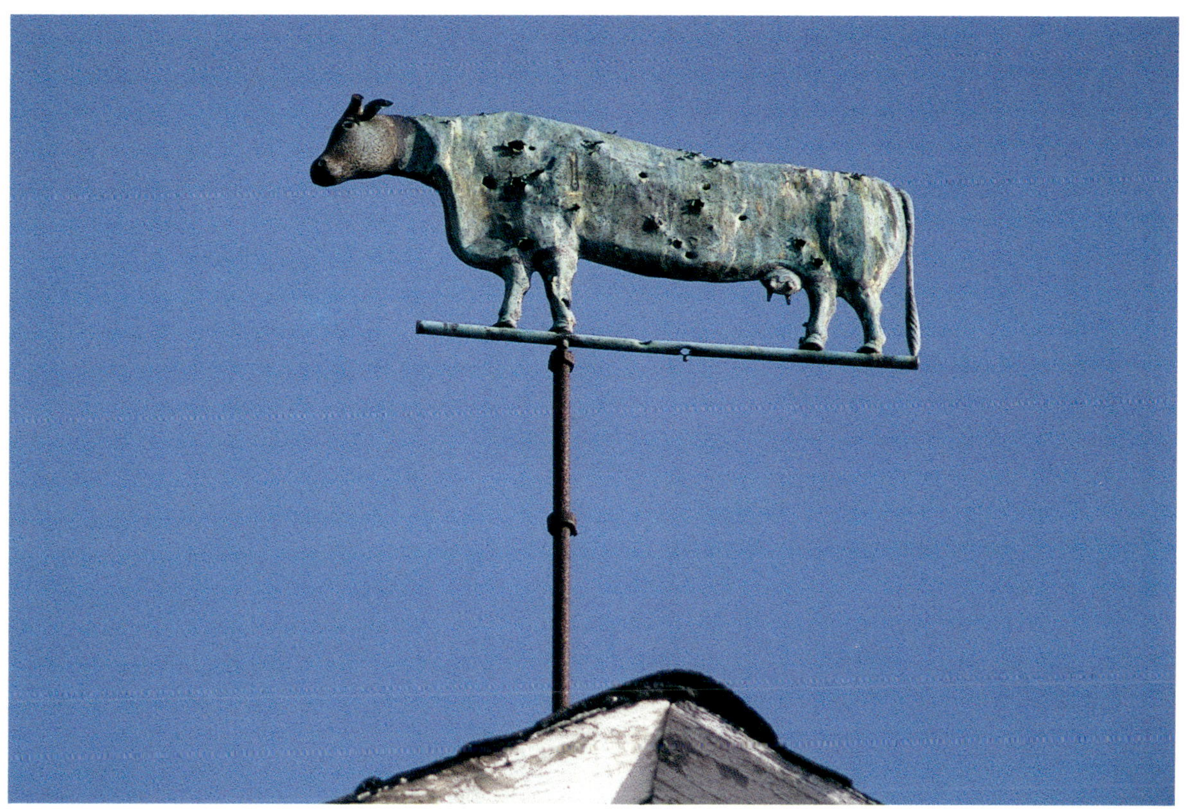

This is a good example of how humor can contribute to the creative process. Is it a bull, or is it a cow? Both! The owner explained to me that he wanted a cow vane for his roof. However, since he particularly liked the mold of a bull, he persuaded the vane maker to alter the form somewhat. The result is what he describes as a bull in the front and a cow in the back.

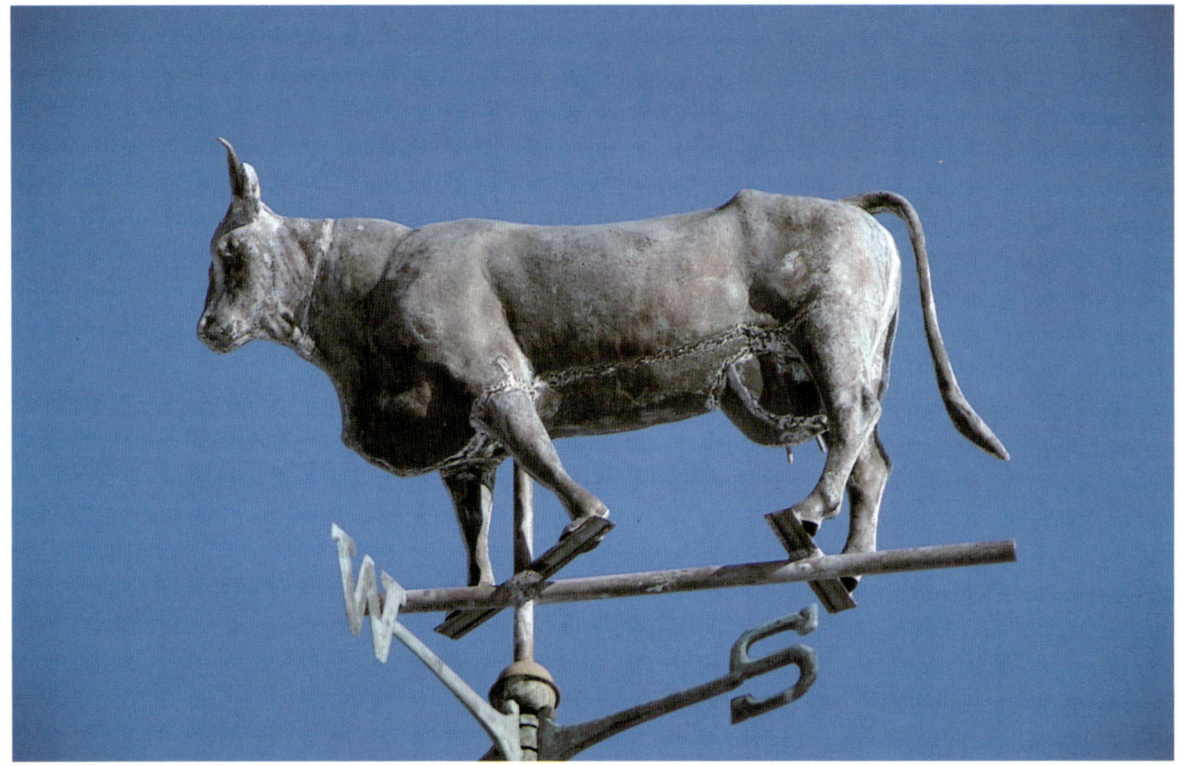

The grasshopper historically has been a symbol of exchange, signaling a trading center to shipping merchants and seamen. It also signified Old World finance. The most famous weather vane of all is a 1742 grasshopper made by Deacon Shem Drowne, which is still mounted on top of Boston's Faneuil Hall. The contemporary grasshopper shown here is perched on a home.

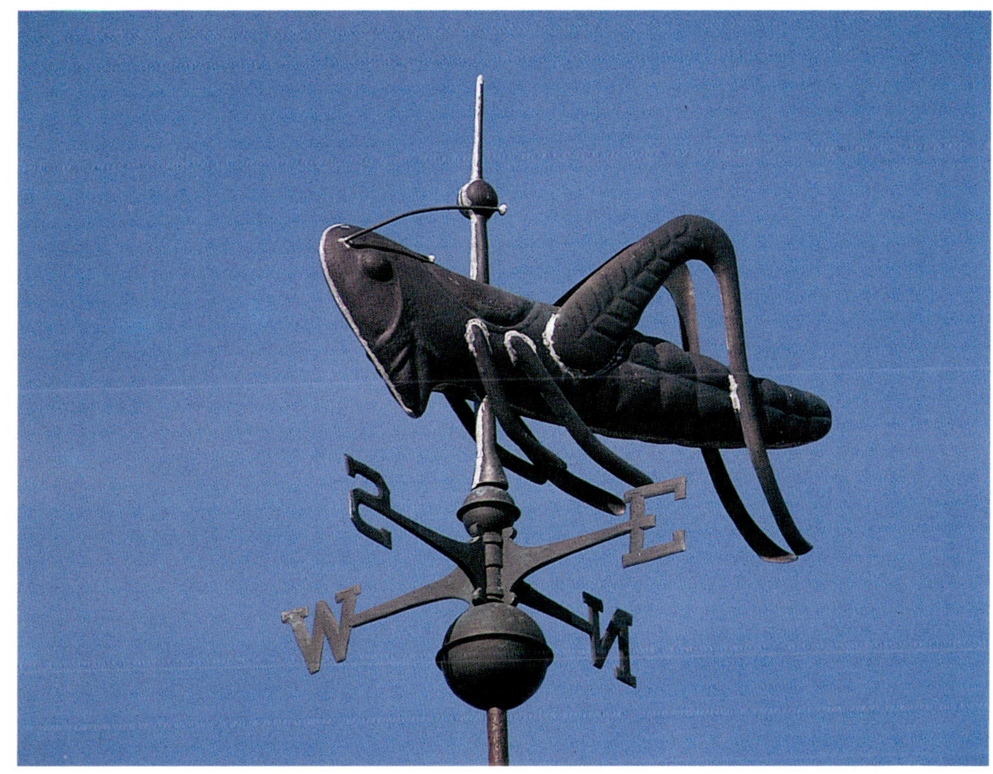

The First Parish Unitarian Church of Kennebunk has an unusual vane. This ear of corn is a painted bronze copy that replaced the original, heavily damaged, wooden one. The first part of the church was built in 1772, and major renovations, including the addition of the bell tower, were made in 1803. Local housewright Thomas Eaton, responsible for the 1803 work, was greatly influenced by renowned Boston architect Asher Benjamin (1773–1845), who wrote The Country Builder's Assistant, *published in 1797. Eaton obviously designed the tower, right down to the ear of corn weather vane, from Plate 33 in Benjamin's book. This explains the presence of such an unusual theme for a vane in a seafaring town. The ear of corn may signify fertility or harvest.*

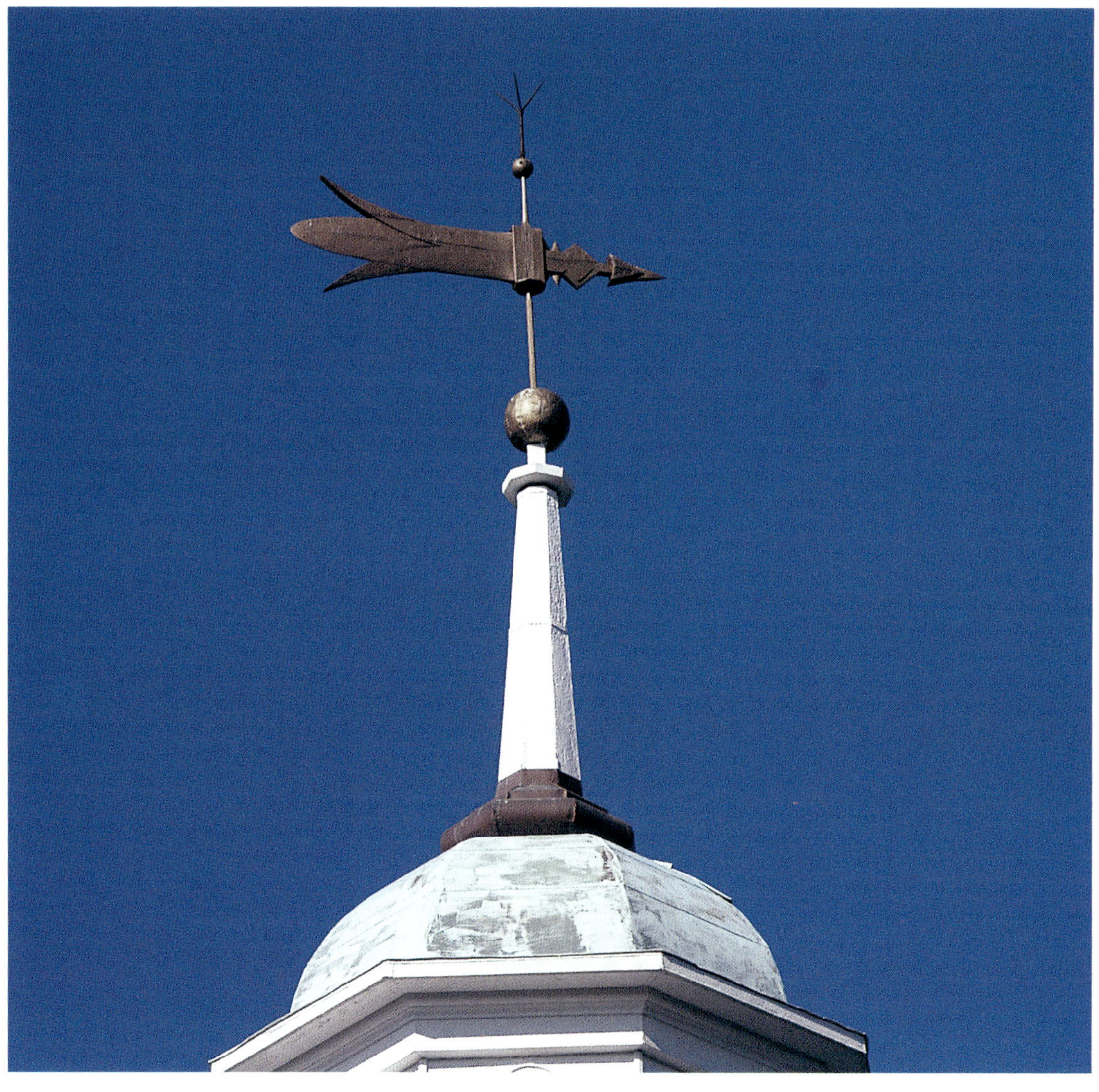

A contemporary dove with olive branch made by craftsman Gilman B. Whitman graces the Southport Methodist Church. One of the church members had this made in memory of her late husband.

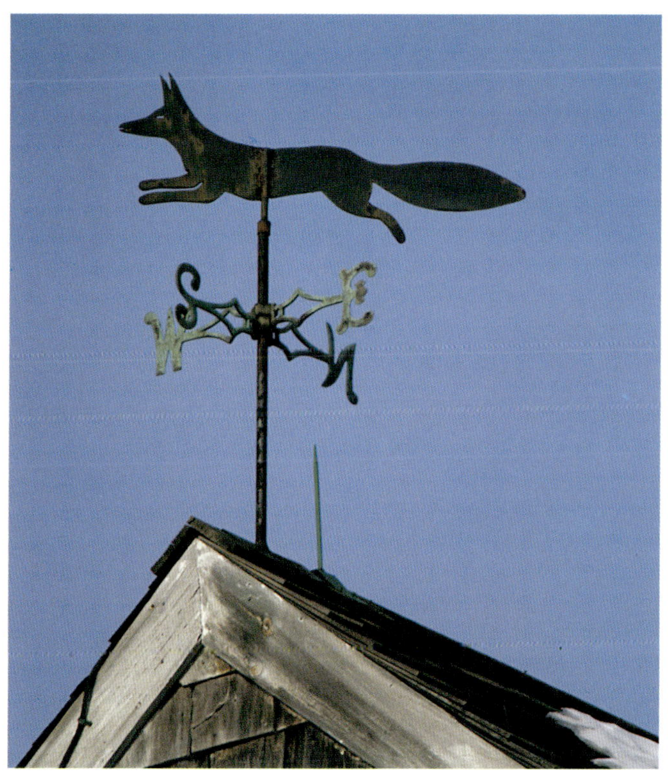

Weather vanes are sometimes altered to create a new subject. This contemporary fox was redesigned by the owner from a horse vane and made by a local blacksmith. Foxes are occasionally seen on the owner's property, providing the inspiration for her new design.

A new copper moose strolls across the sky. Wildlife subjects have always been popular for weather vanes.

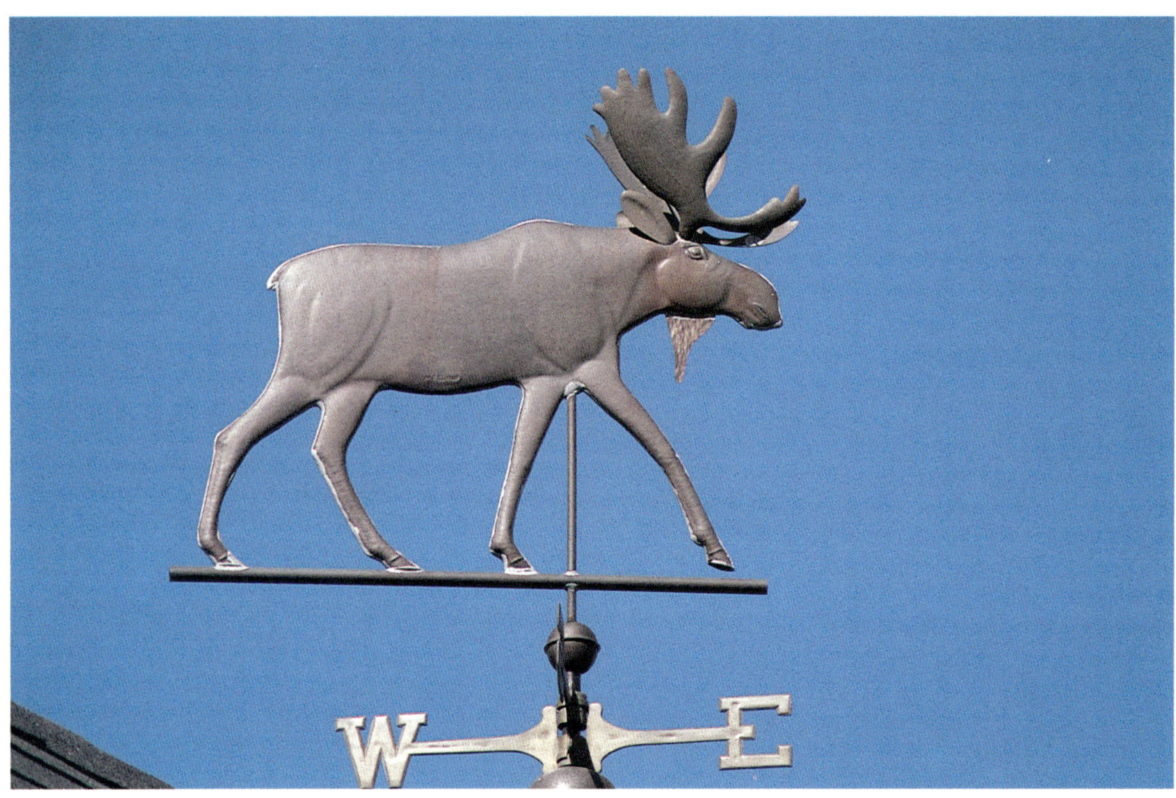

A leaping deer provides an elegant wildlife theme. This is another twentieth-century vane.

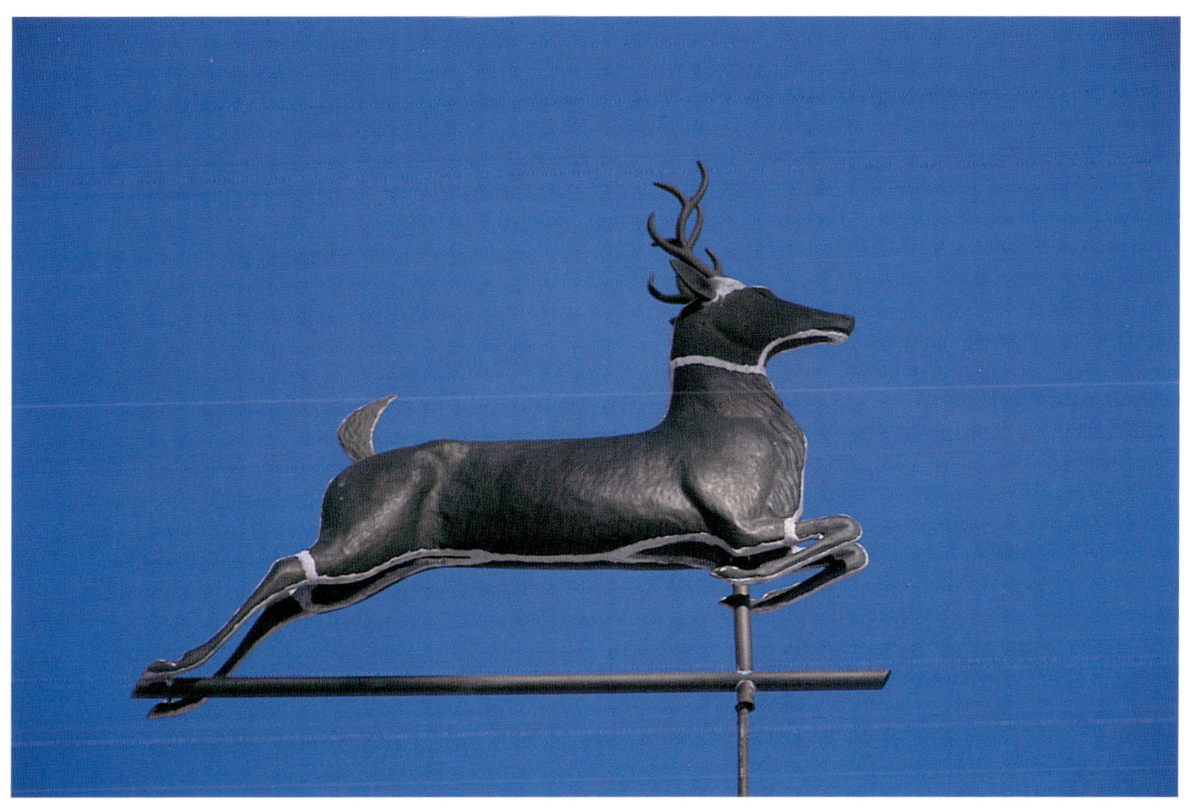

This new sturgeon found on the Kennebec Journal *building in Gardiner is a symbol for the entire town. The Kennebec Indians, who originally inhabited the area, found sturgeon in great abundance at the mouth of what they called Cabbassa ("place to catch sturgeon") on the Kennebec River. Export of sturgeon to England was an important source of livelihood for the early settlers.*

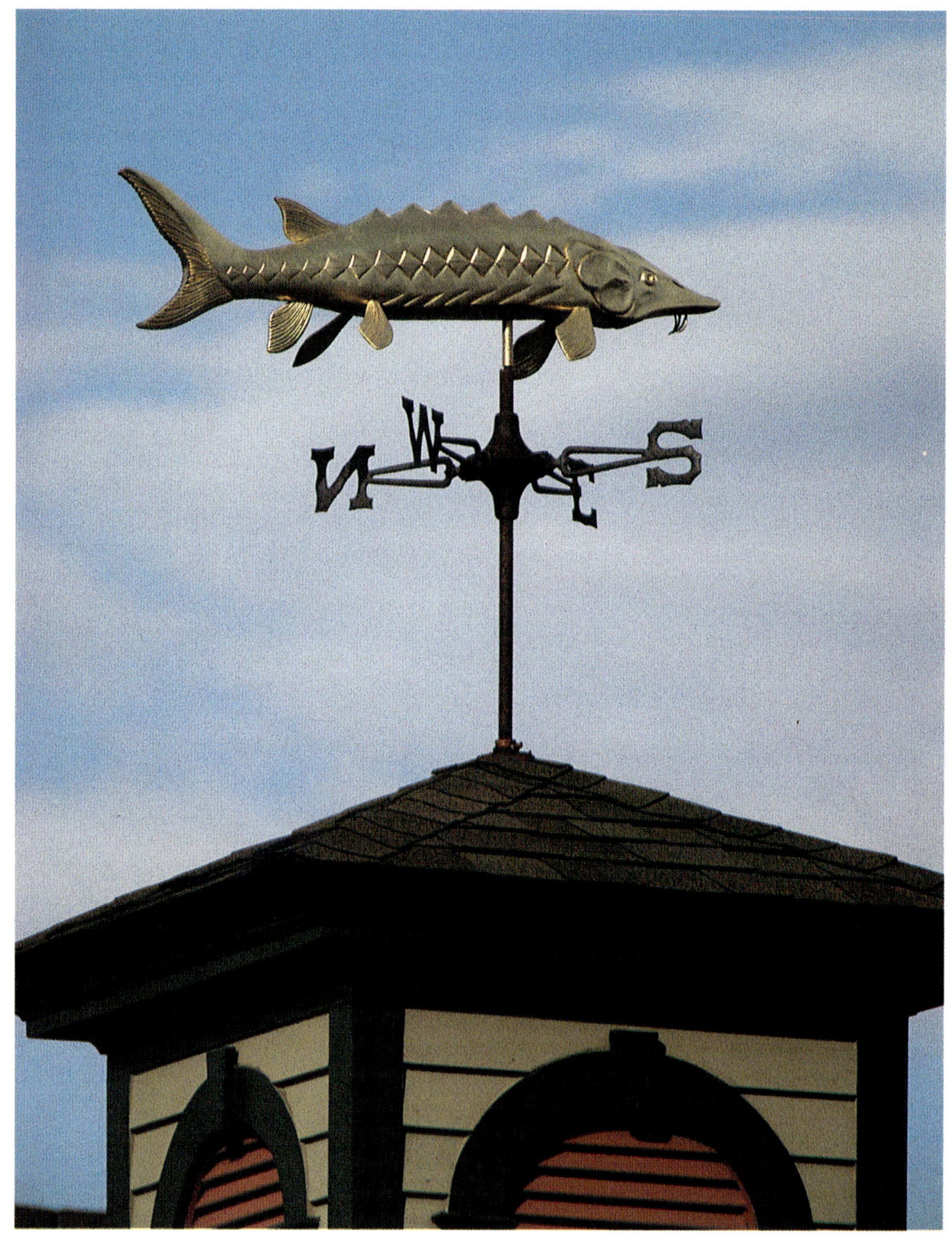

A copper fish is appropriately sited on a home overlooking the sea. It dates from the late nineteenth or early twentieth century.

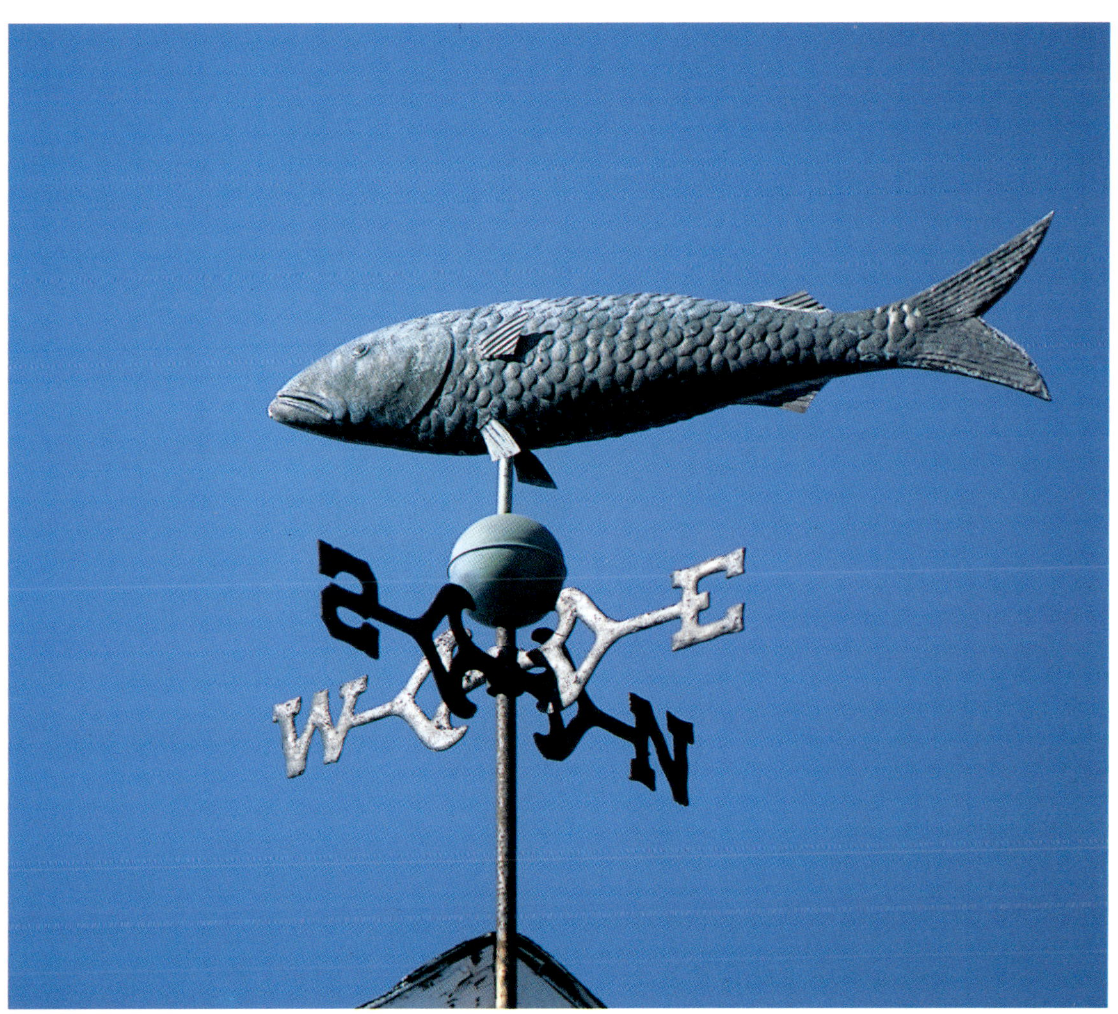

This swordfish looks to be a 1920s or 1930s sheet-metal silhouette that is reminiscent of a design popular in the early 1800s. The swordfish's graceful lines are ideal for piercing the wind.

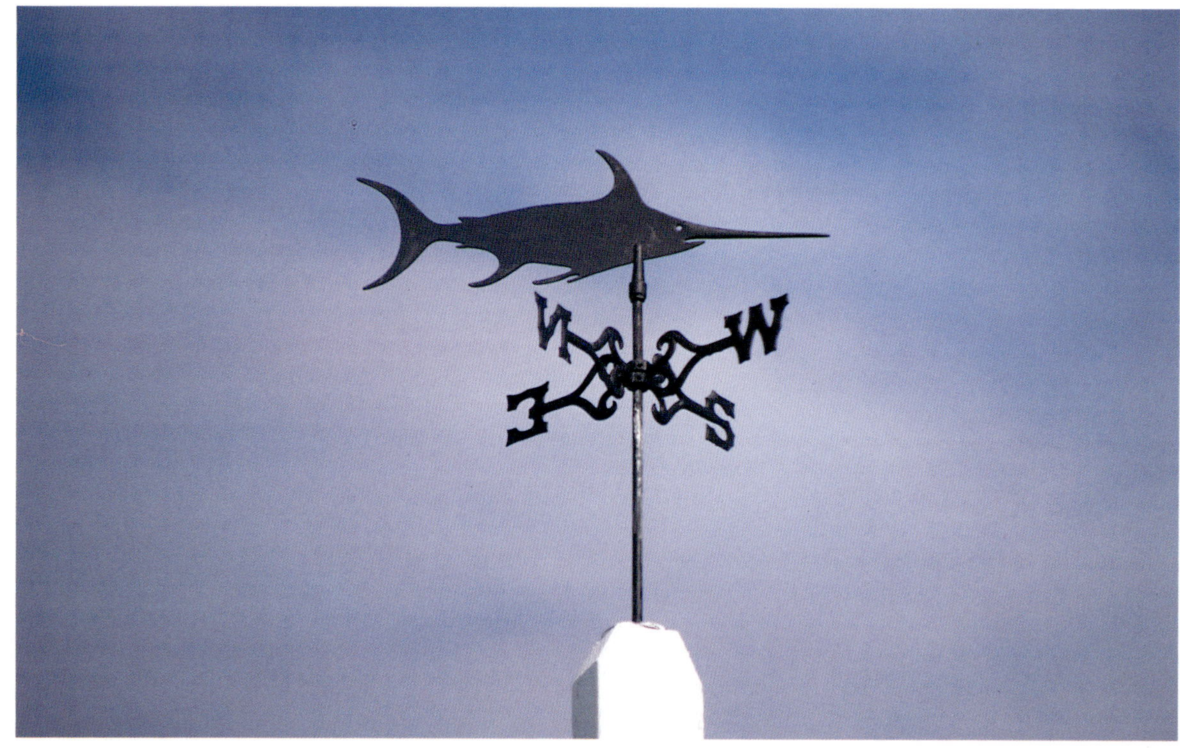

A Midwestern artist designed this contemporary sperm whale for his Maine friends. The circular design on the post offers an intriguing setting for the vane.

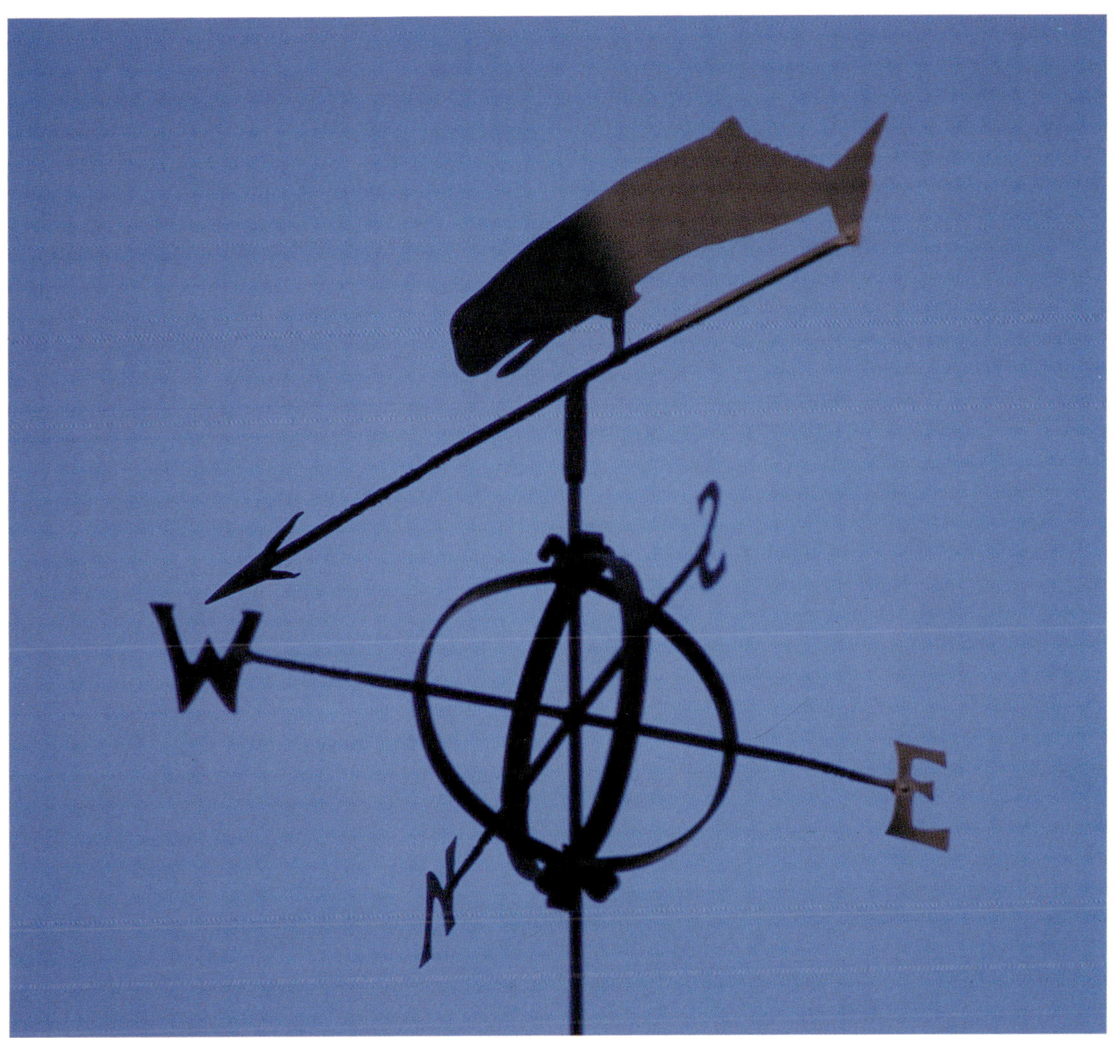

A book of Maine's weather vanes would not be complete without a lobster vane. This one is on the Rockland fire station, which was dedicated in 1971.

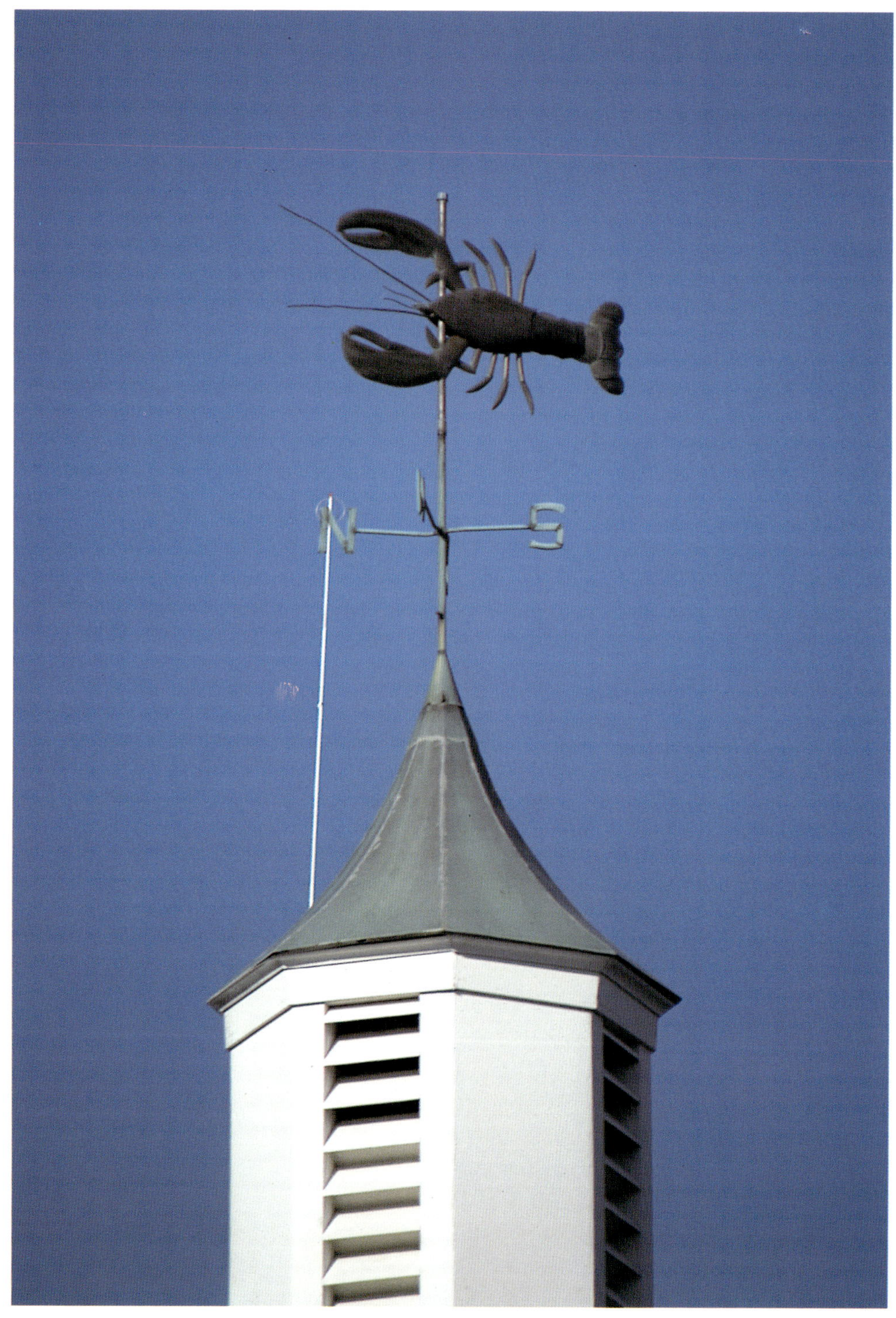

I was standing in snow up to my knees enjoying the attention of a curious horse when I photographed this mid-twentieth-century whale vane. It seems to be a fairly accurate design, although the tail flukes are in a vertical rather than horizontal position. The vertical style probably reduces resistance and allows the vane to respond more accurately to the wind.

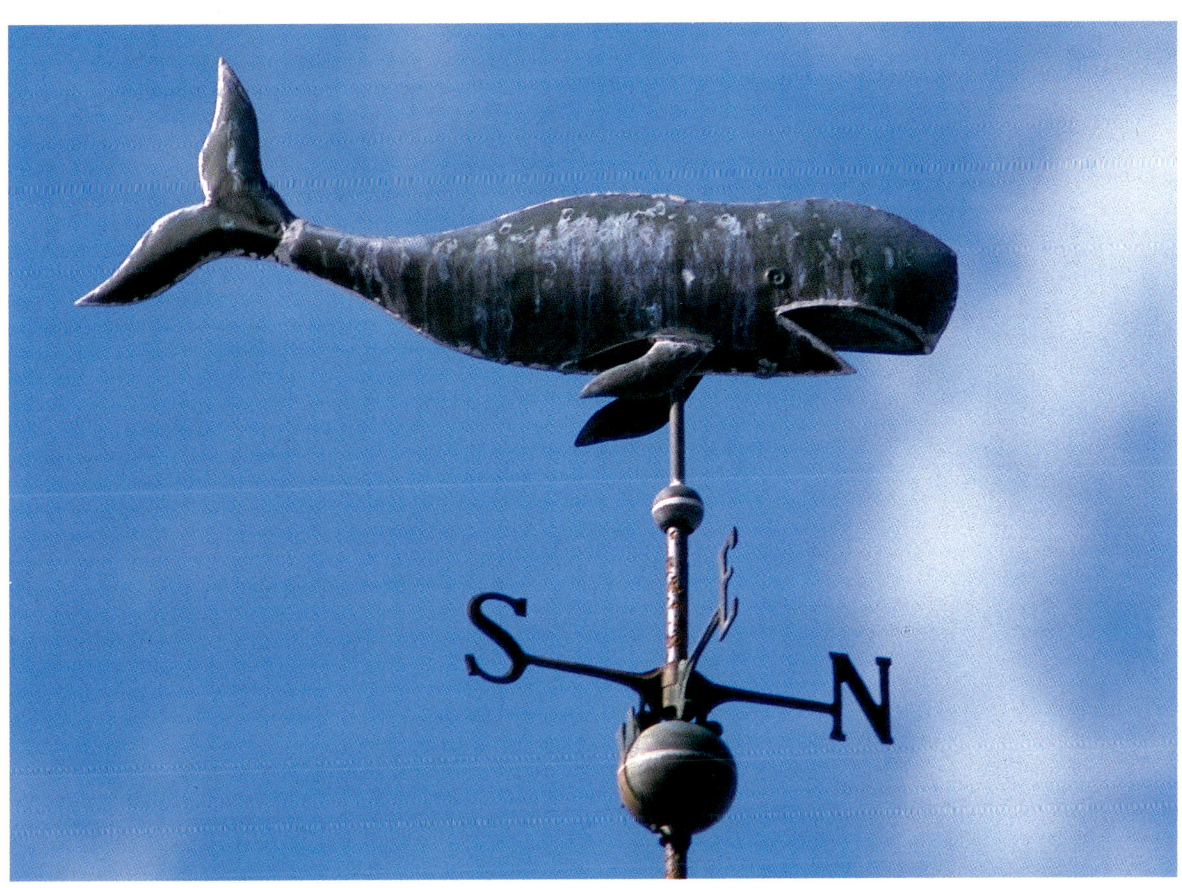

The sea captain seems to be pointing the way through a calm clear day at sea in this copy of an 1840s vane. It sits on a Kennebunkport antique shop right at the water's edge where it still can point to sea.

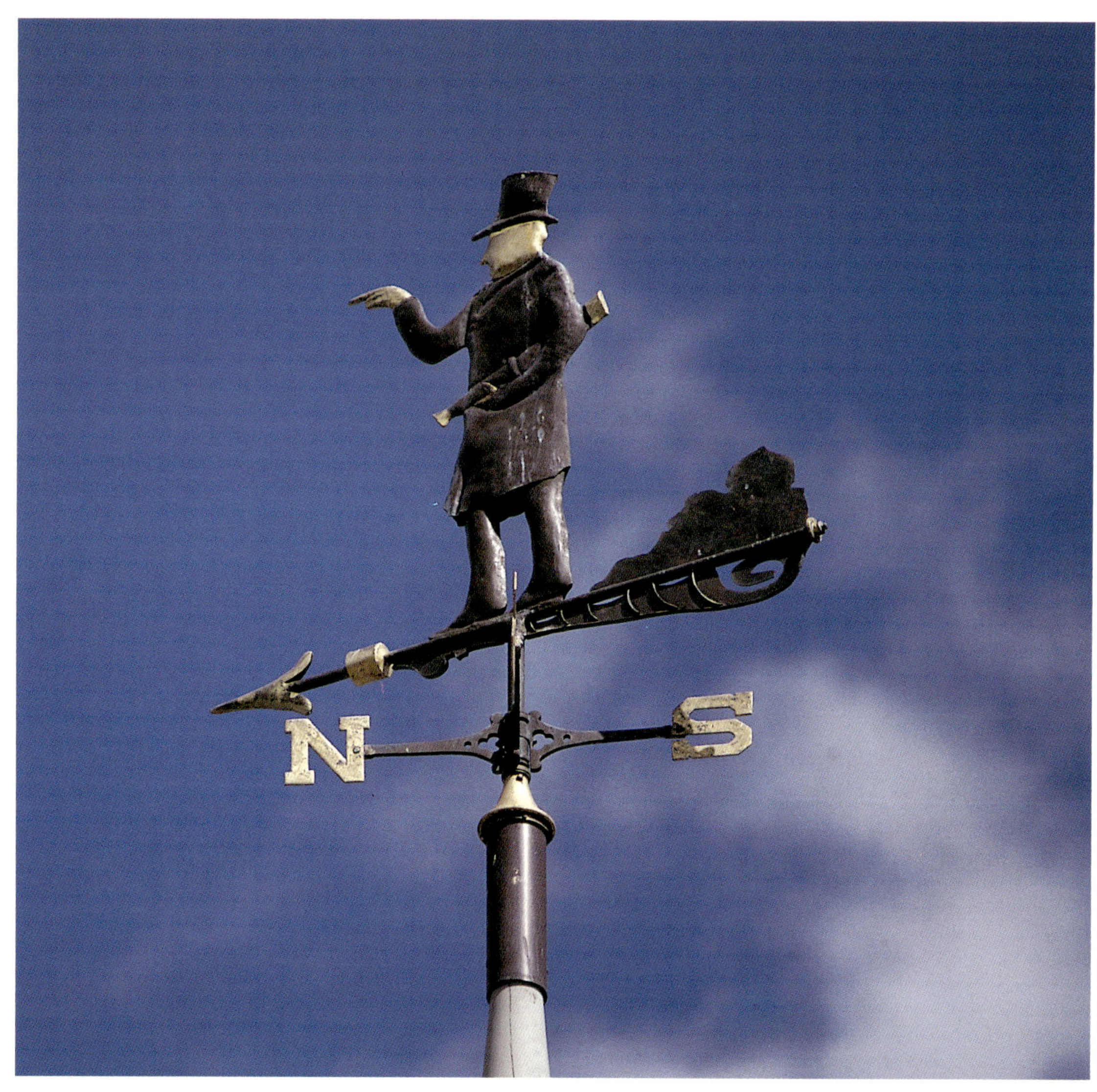

Ships and the Sea

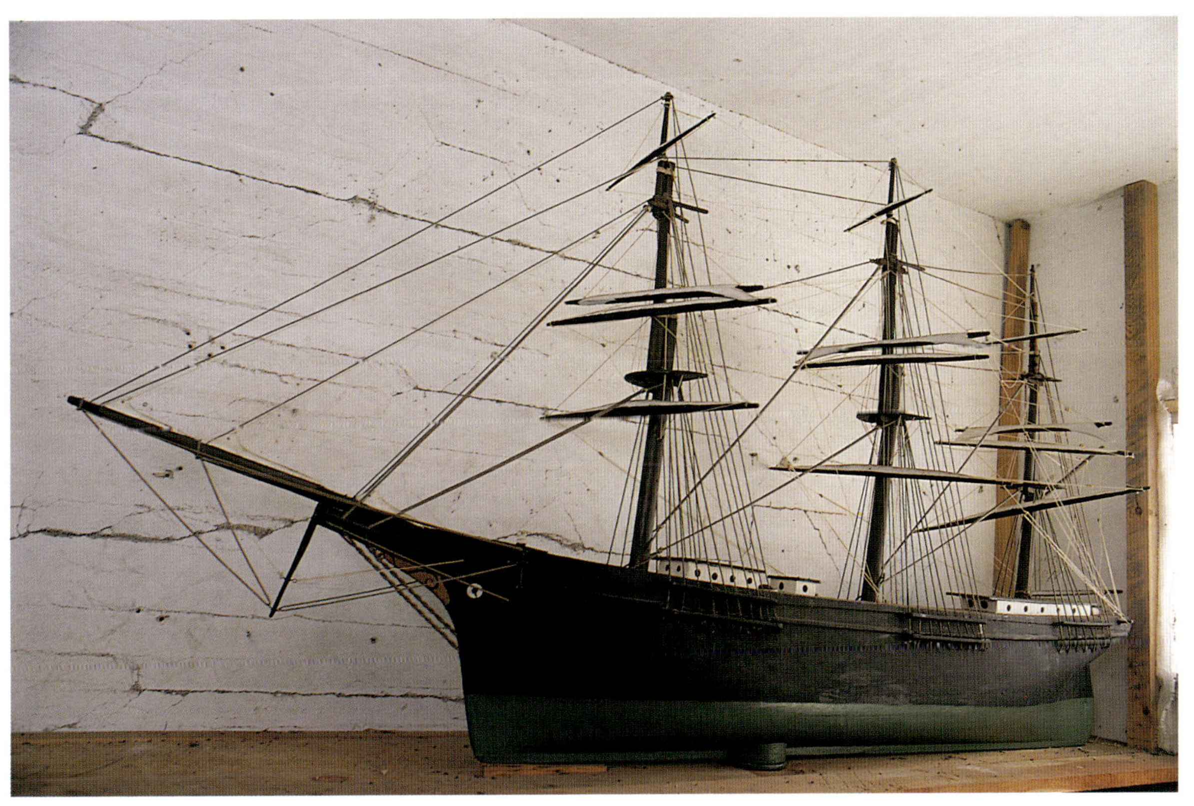

Preceding page: *This noble merchant vessel vane represents wonderful craftsmanship, history, and one family's long maritime heritage. Its massive, solid wood hull measures eight feet from stern to bowsprit, with a twenty-two-inch beam. From keel to mast top, it stands forty-one inches tall. The strong lines, intricate rigging, and attention to detail make it a commanding sight.*

It has special meaning for its owner's family because it provides a link through the generations. The elderly owner's grandfather, a builder of merchant vessels, carved it in the mid 1800s. The present owner, a former lighthouse keeper for thirty-five years, can remember it sitting on top of his barn when he was a young child. To protect it from further weather damage, it was taken down in the early 1900s. A few years ago a son-in-law, who was a member of the Merchant Marines, put a fresh coat of paint on it and replaced the rigging.

For security reasons it is now bolted to a workbench in a barn on the same property where it hung years ago.

The branches of a tree frame a 1930s sailing ship vane perched on a post that has been bent with time. Billowy clouds offer a nice backdrop to the graceful lines of the silhouette.

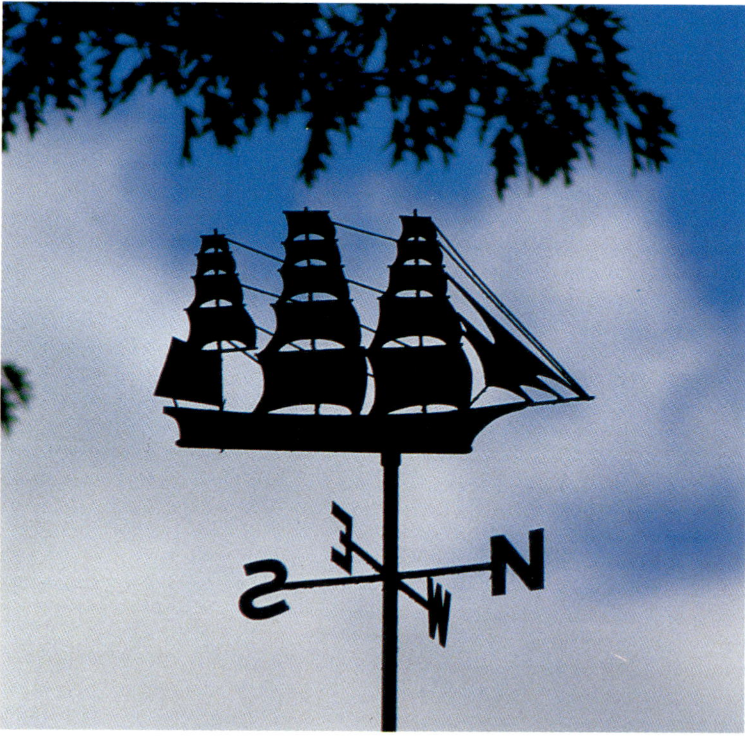

The copper sloop weather vane on Miller Library at Colby College, in Waterville, was hung in 1939. It is a replica of the sloop Hero, *which brought the Reverend Jeremiah Chaplin, Colby's founder, from Boston to Kennebec. When school officials decided to put a weather vane on the tower, they hired a well-known marine architect of the time, H.I. Chapelle, to create the design. After studying pictures, Chapelle drew* Hero *to scale, but to achieve proper balance and resistance to the wind, he modified the design by adding more jibs and topsails. Thus, it is a more glamorous version of the real working sloop.*

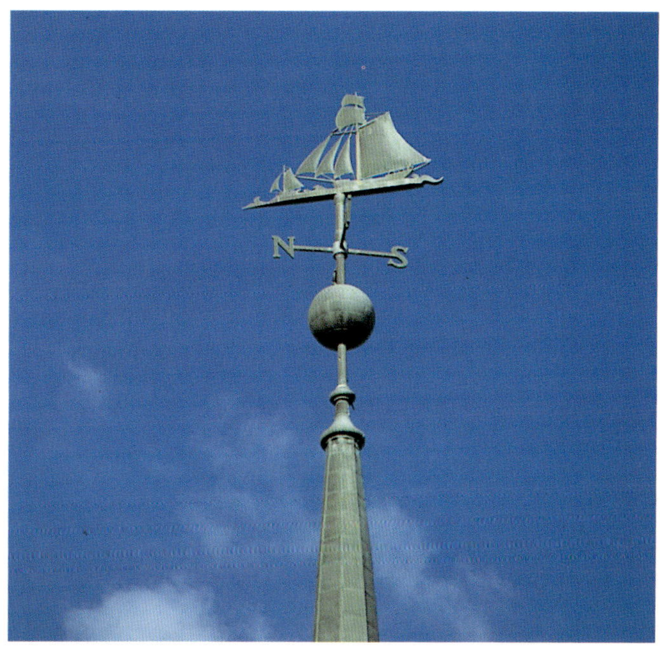

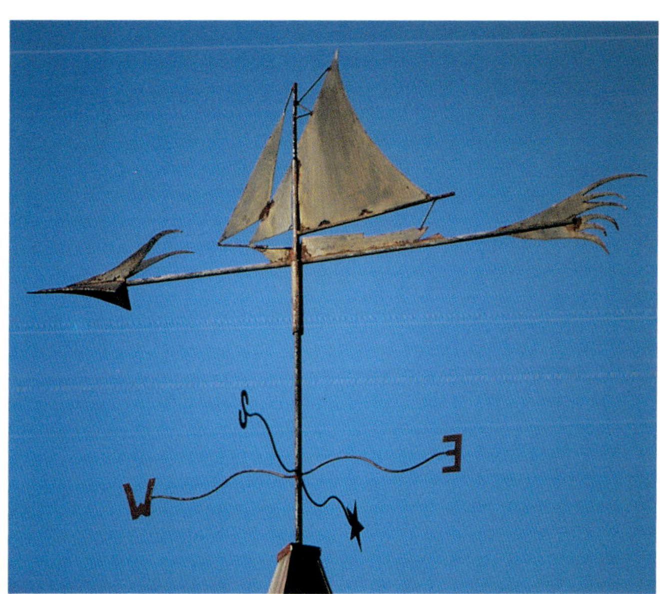

Pride in local history played a part in the conception and design of this Friendship sloop on a bank in Stonington. When Jack Hemenway was asked to create a vane with a nautical design in keeping with Deer Isle's heritage, he decided to do a copy of the old locally made Friendship sloop Dictator. *He worked from photographs, and to be doubly sure of accuracy he asked a man who had actually worked on* Dictator *to confirm that all was "seaworthy" before welding the pieces together. Having never made one before, Hemenway unfortunately made the vane too heavy, so he replaced the original vane with a copy made of lighter metal. The second vane, hung in 1974, is the one shown here. The wavy directionals add interest.*

The well-known gilded galleon that has flown over Portland City Hall since 1904 was taken down for restoration in 1990. It represents the vessels of the early explorers, and a glimpse of it riding high above the Portland skyline takes the viewer back to an earlier time.

Portland City Hall was designed by the prestigious New York architects Carrére and Hastings, and Carrére himself designed the weather vane. It is made of gilded sheet copper formed over a wood frame and measures eight feet at its longest and highest points.

The restoration was done by Kezar Falls, Maine, craftsman Roger Lawrence and his wife, Debra. The photograph was taken shortly before the vane was returned to Portland. Over a thousand squares of gold leaf were required to cover this vast piece, each painstakingly applied to a surface pitted from years of exposure to the elements.

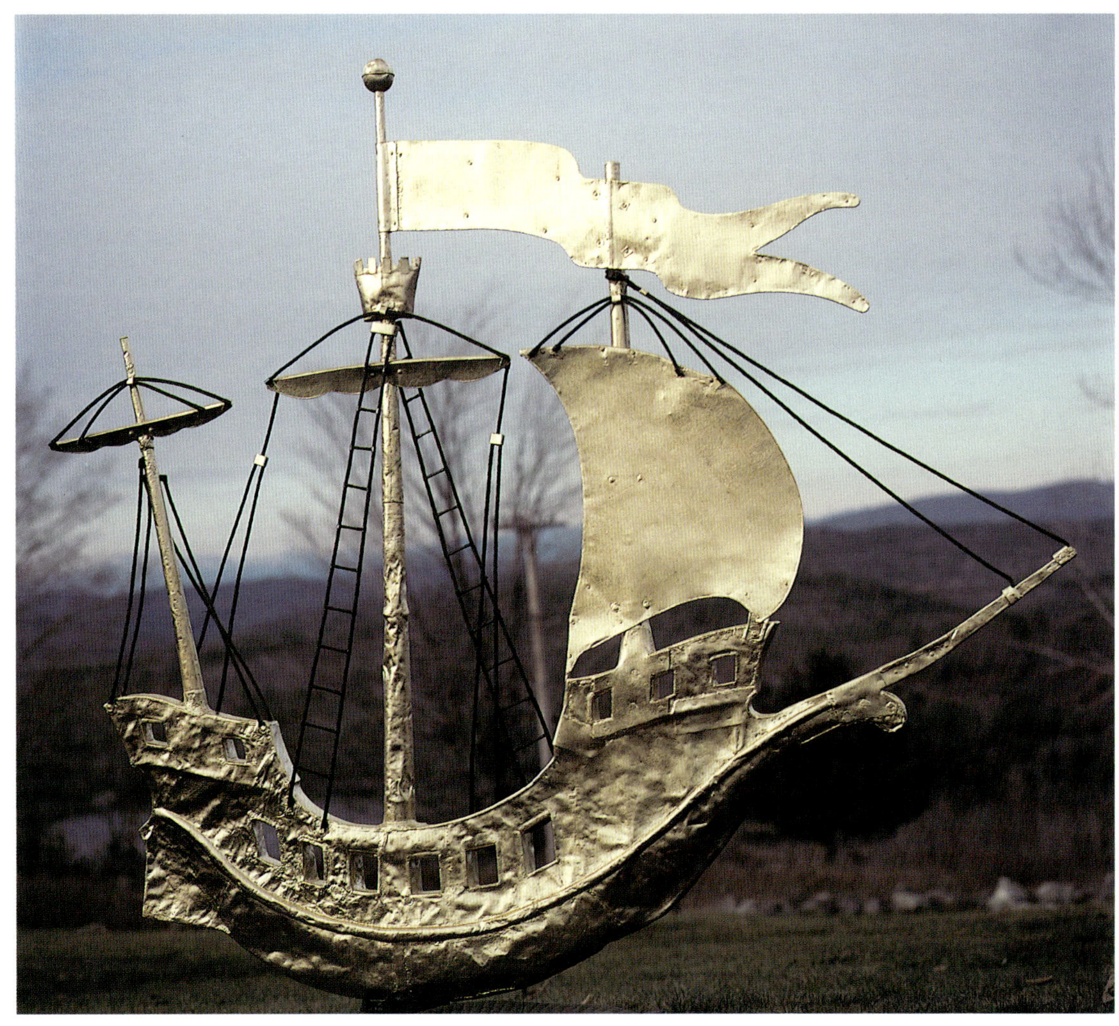

Waldoboro is called "the home of the five-masted schooner." These massive vessels were built there on the Medomak River between 1870 and 1908, and were known as the Palmer fleet. This five-masted schooner silhouette vane is mounted on a Waldoboro bank.

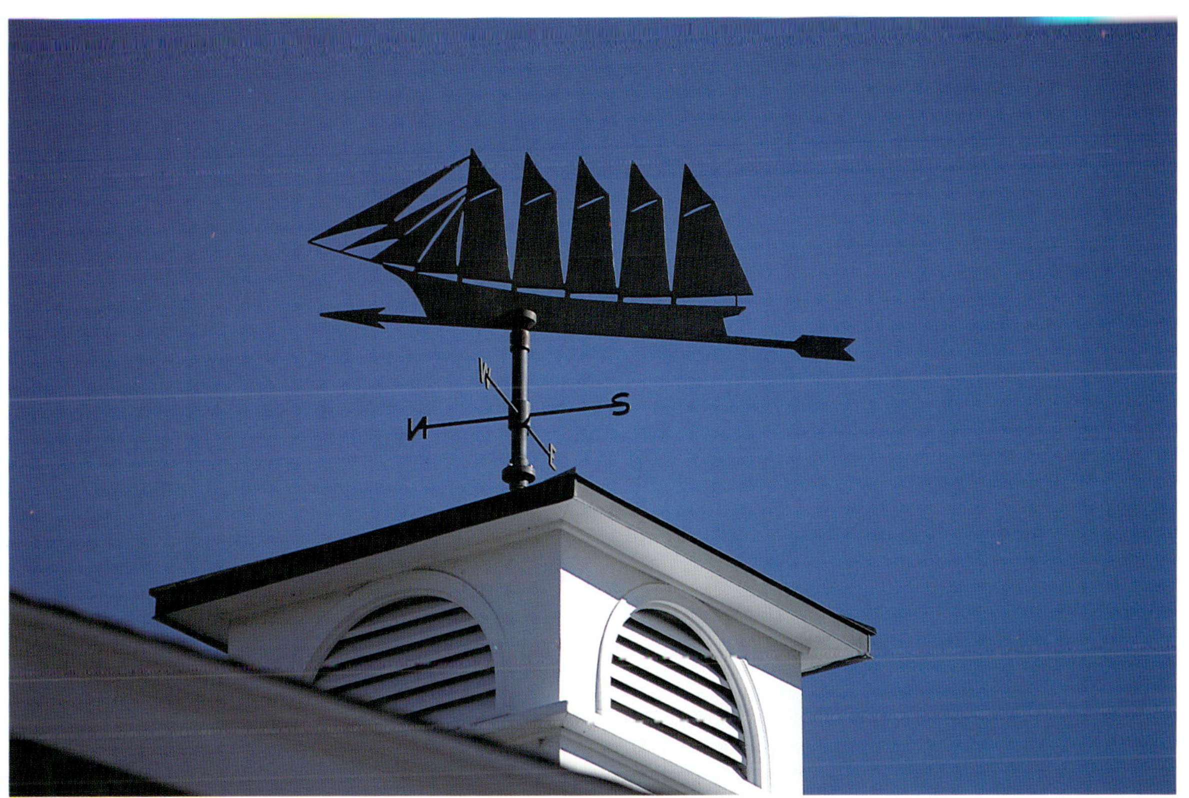

A relatively new ship weather vane makes a commanding presence on a Damariscotta bank. The elegant gold leaf radiates warmth.

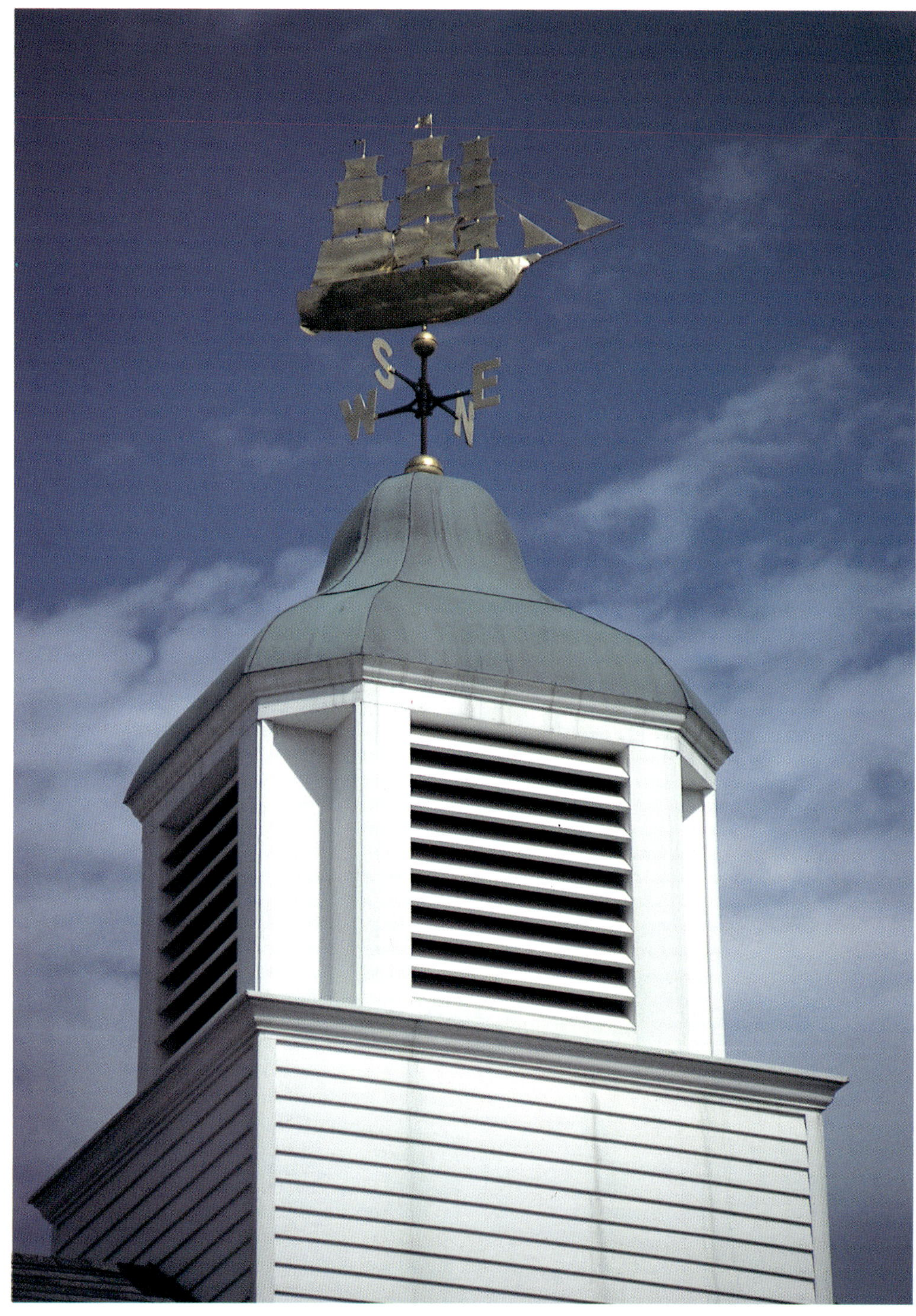

The combination of the white clouds, white church, and white schooner vane provided a delightful sight as I was driving through Boothbay Harbor, where this twentieth-century vane tops the United Methodist Church.

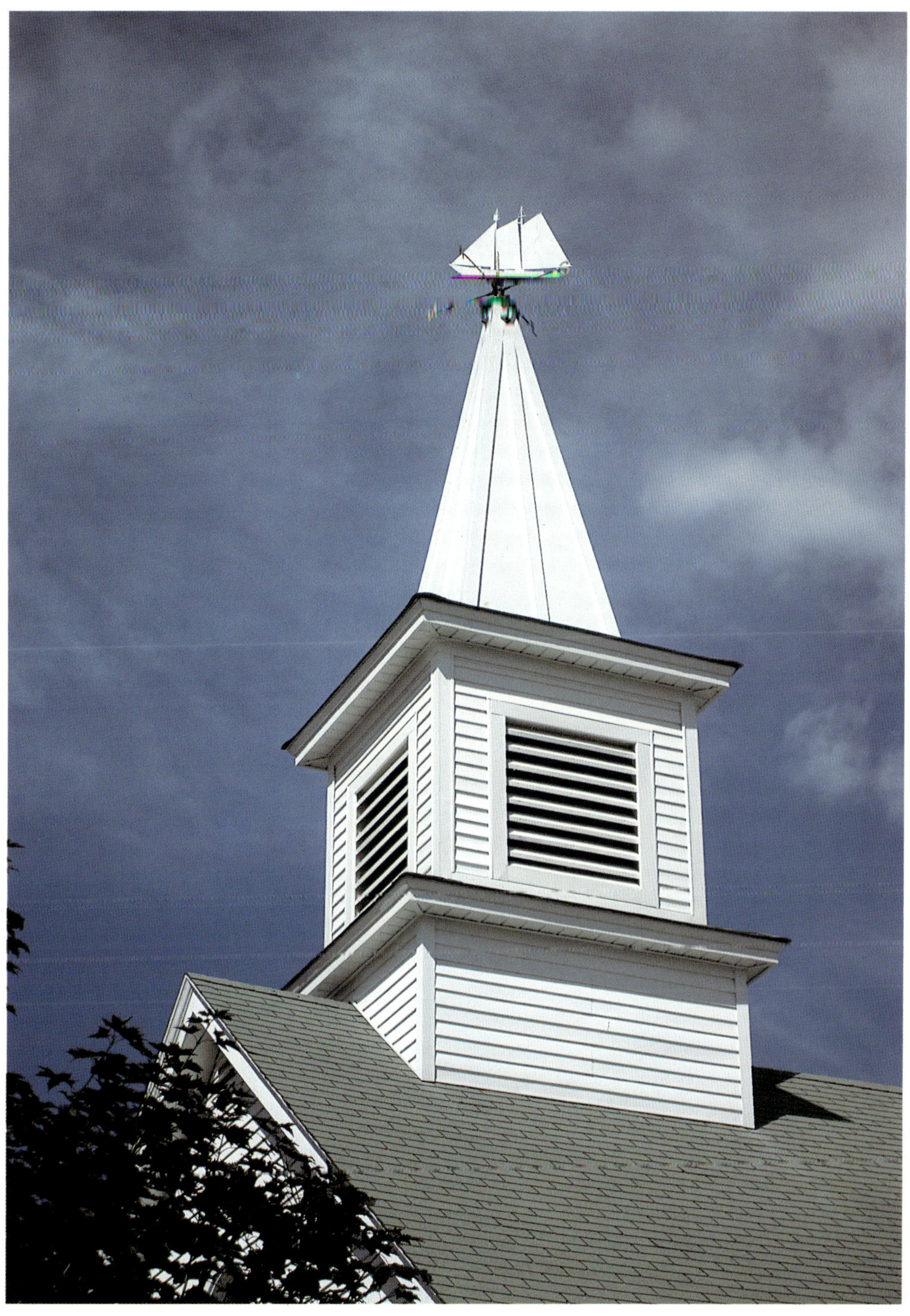

A nicely shaped twentieth-century sailboat vane sails above a southern Maine business.

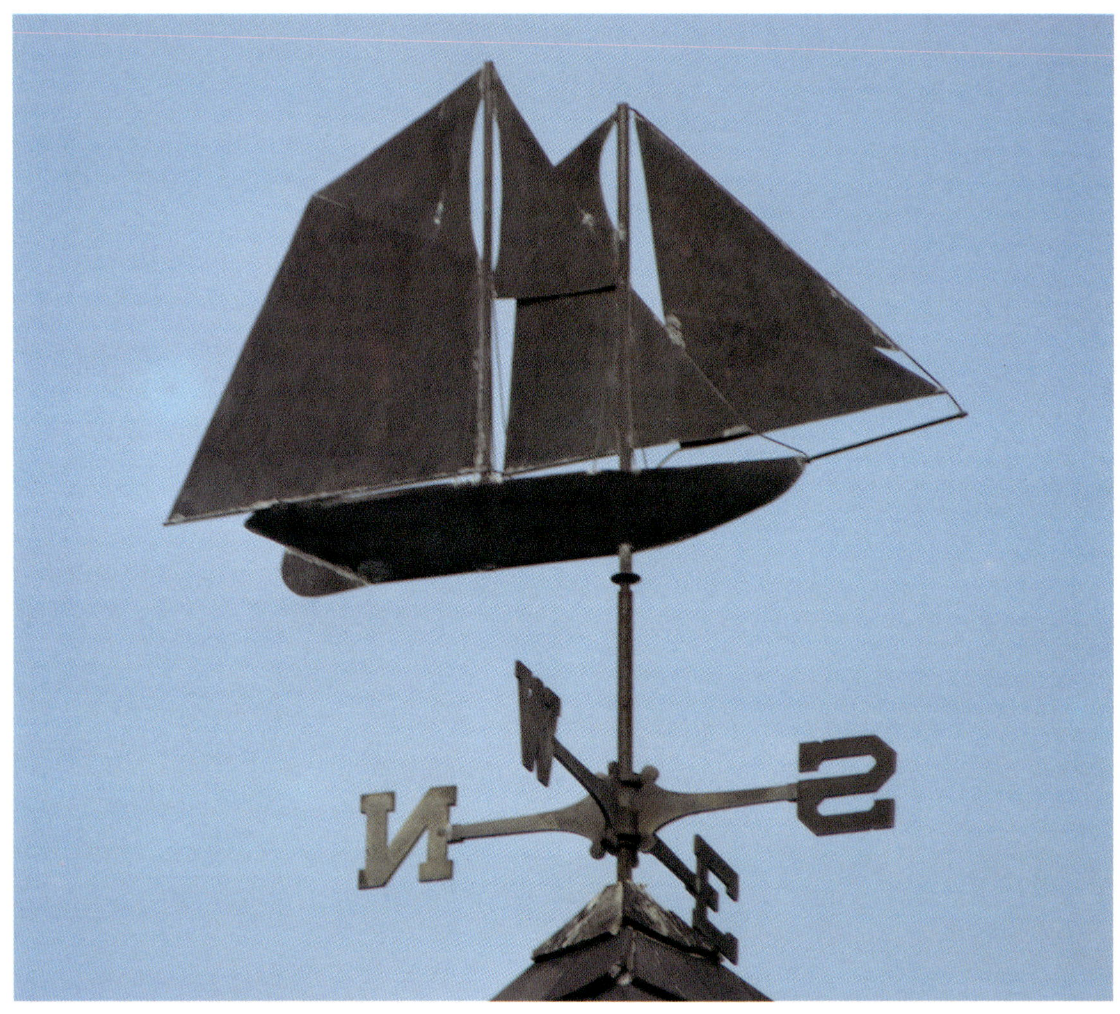

This three-dimensional sailboat, the handiwork of the owner and his father, was built in 1959. The hull and masts are solid wood, and the sail is stainless steel. Copper wire was used for the rigging. The vane is taken down every winter to protect it from the winds and ice, and its reappearance on the rooftop announces the arrival of spring.

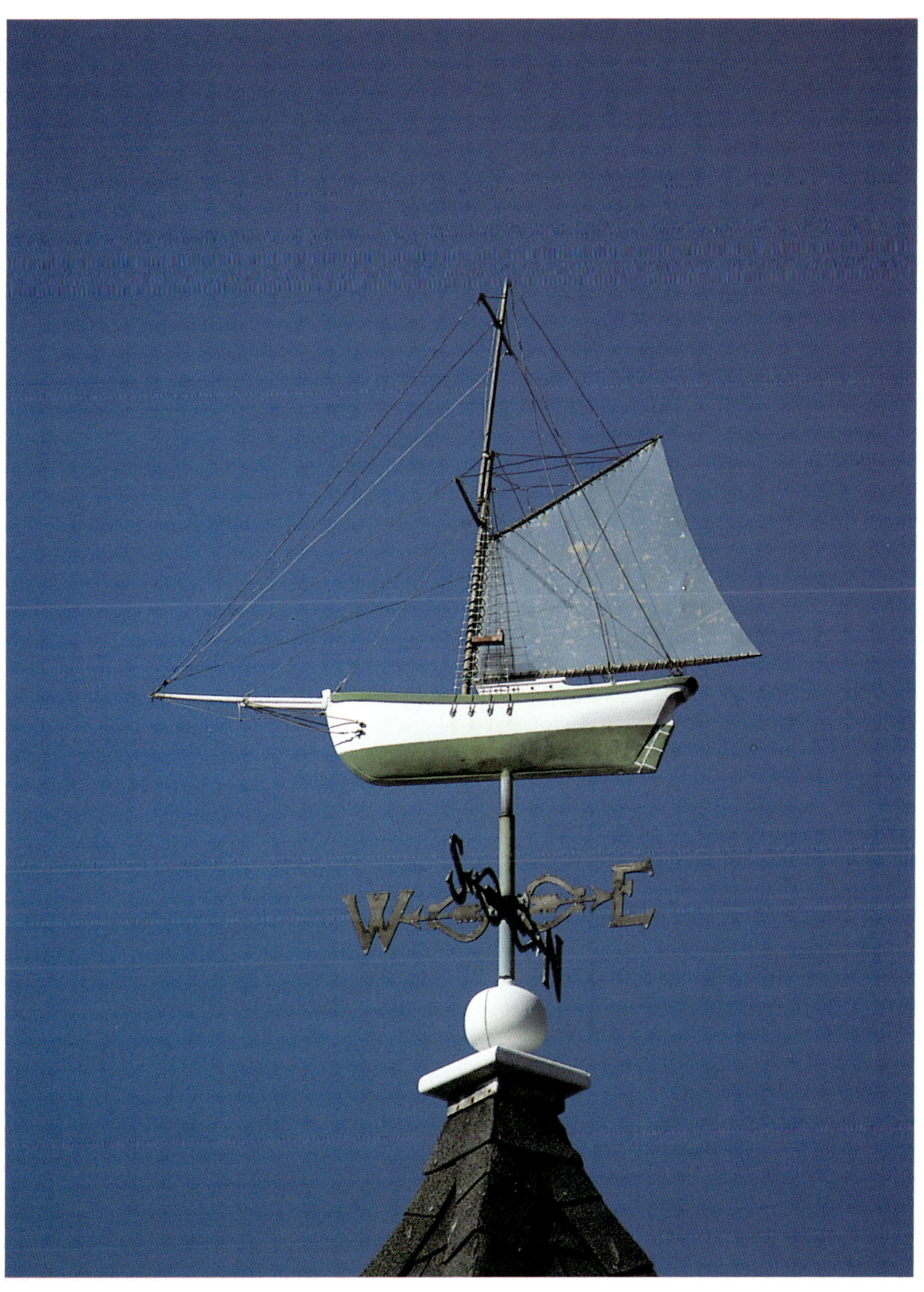

This copper destroyer vane can be seen in Bath at the base of the Route 1 bridge near the Bath Iron Works shipyard. It sits atop the one-story building that formerly was the railroad station. The building (with vane) was dedicated on January 14, 1942. The vane was a gift to the railroad from William S. Newell, who at the time was president of Bath Iron Works. Its design came from the Benson/Gleave class of destroyer, which was under construction at the shipyard during that period. The vane has aged beautifully, and now is covered with a solid green patina.

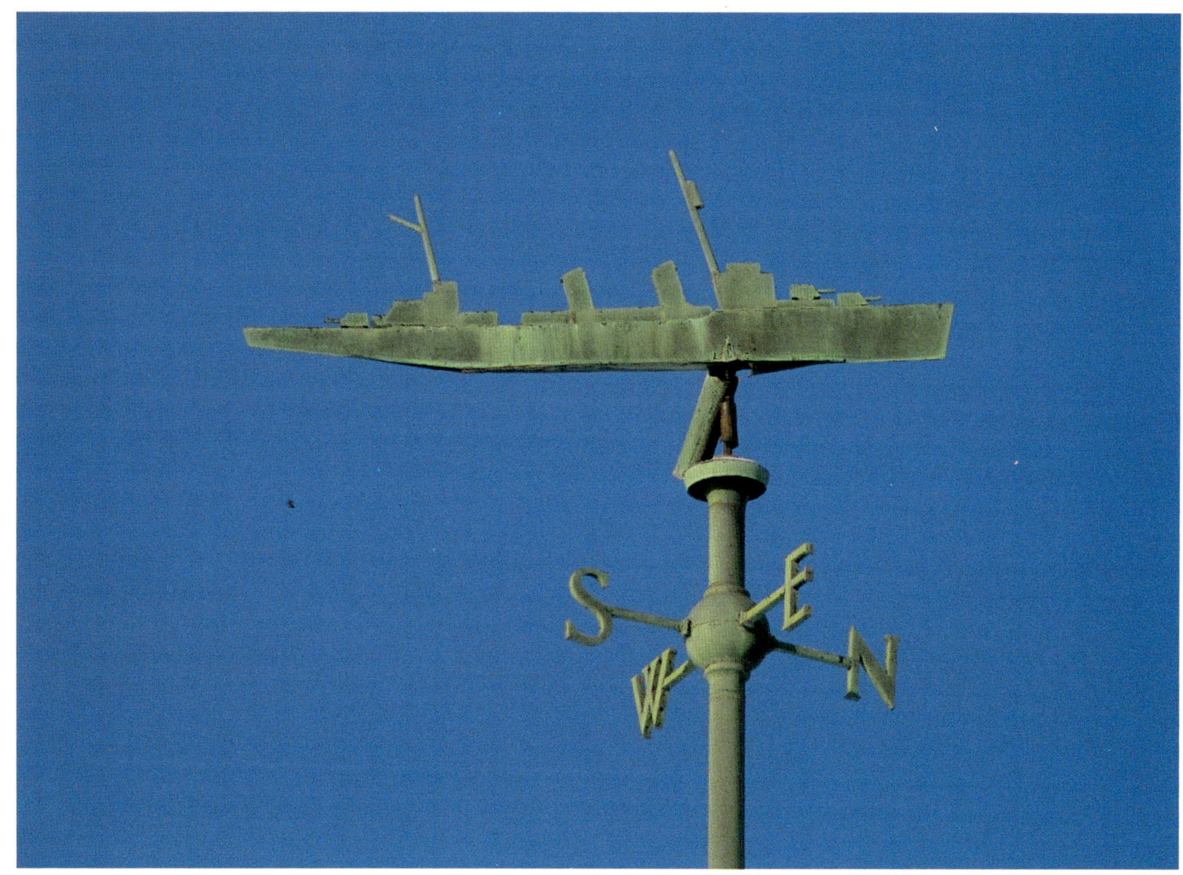

A three-masted copper ship sets atop the Wiscasset fire station. It dates back to the 1930s, giving the surface time to oxidize to its present greenish tone.

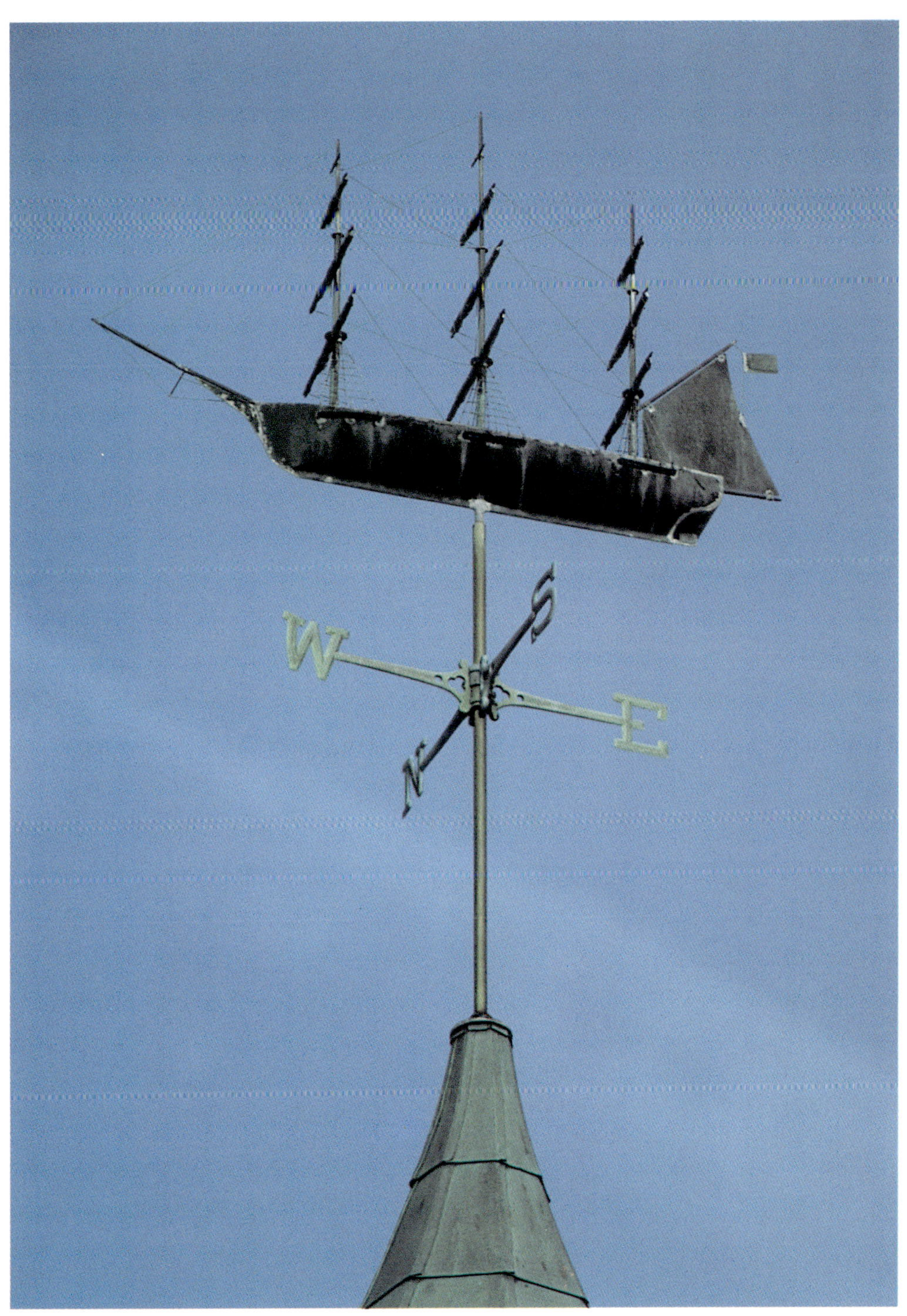

A nicely shaped 1880–1900 sloop sails over Kennebunkport. Fresh gold leaf has been added.

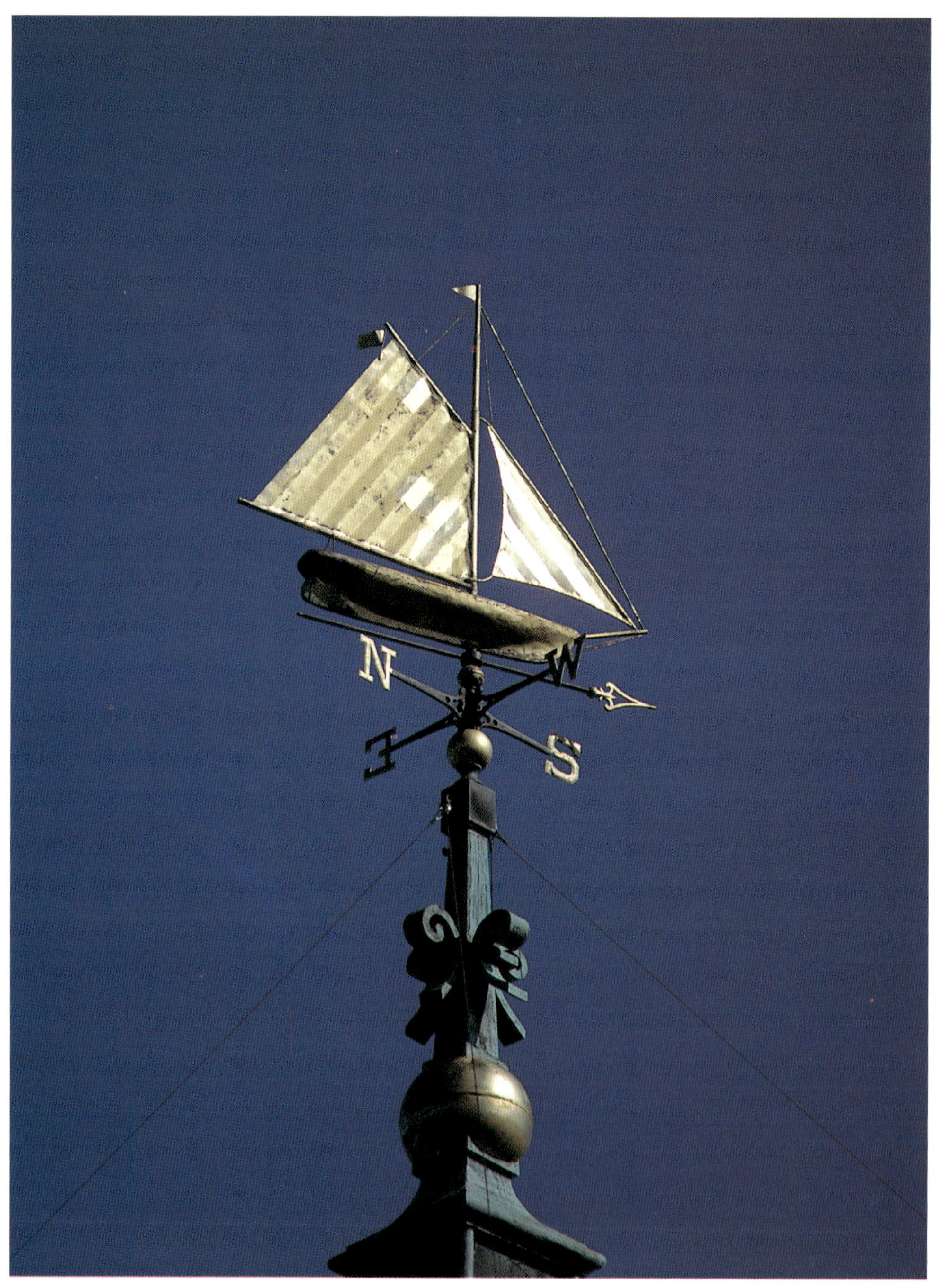

A contemporary copper dory overlooks the ocean from its perch.

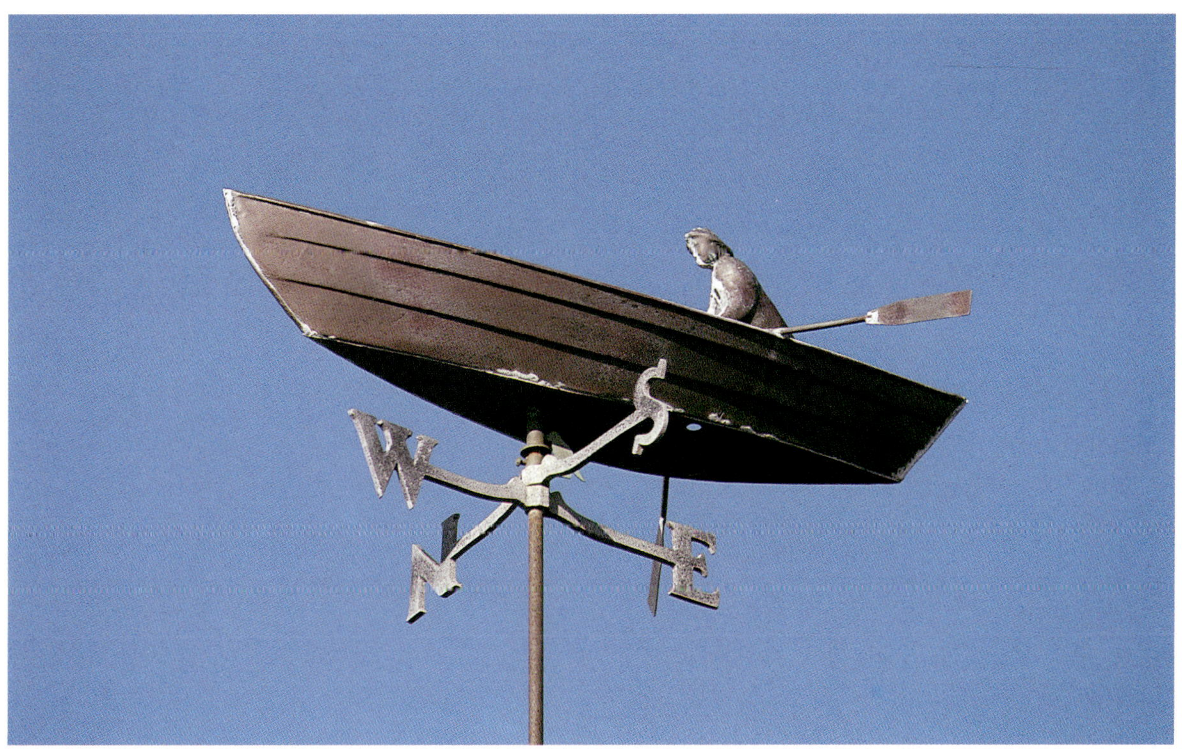

Facing page: *The cut-out details give this wrought iron castle a realistic look. It was made by the owner in 1950.*

Even though most new vanes are either mass-produced or made by professional craftsmen, there are still some to be found that are unique creations of their owners. This appealingly simple one was made out of steel and aluminum as a trade school project.

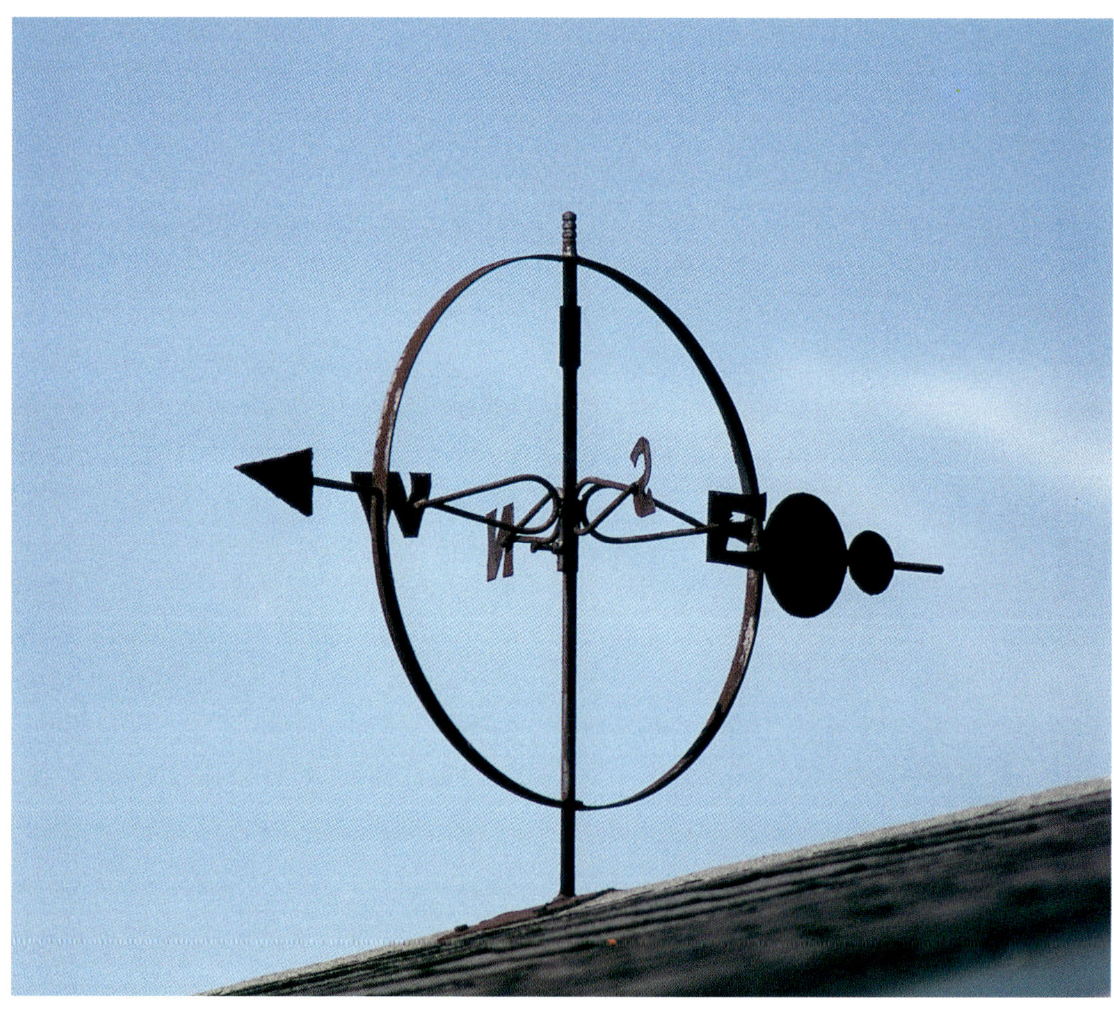

Myth and Symbol

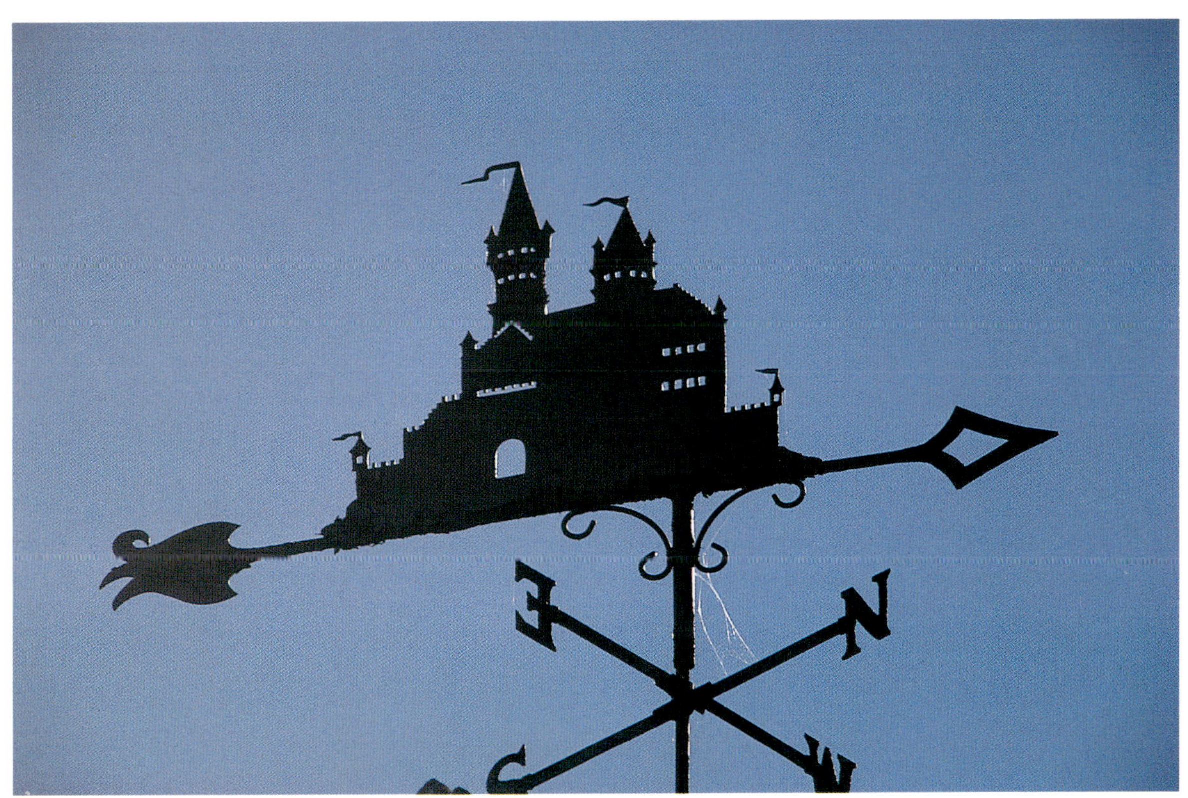

This new wooden mermaid was carved by her owner after the previous rooster vane was stolen. The mermaid theme appealed to him for three reasons: (1) it was a shape that would catch the wind and point properly; (2) his family has a strong affinity for the sea; and (3) they wanted something whimsical. Also, as he points out, no one can say that it doesn't look like a "real" mermaid. Made of laminated white pine and finished with gold colored paint and varnish, it measures forty-two inches from fingertip to tail.

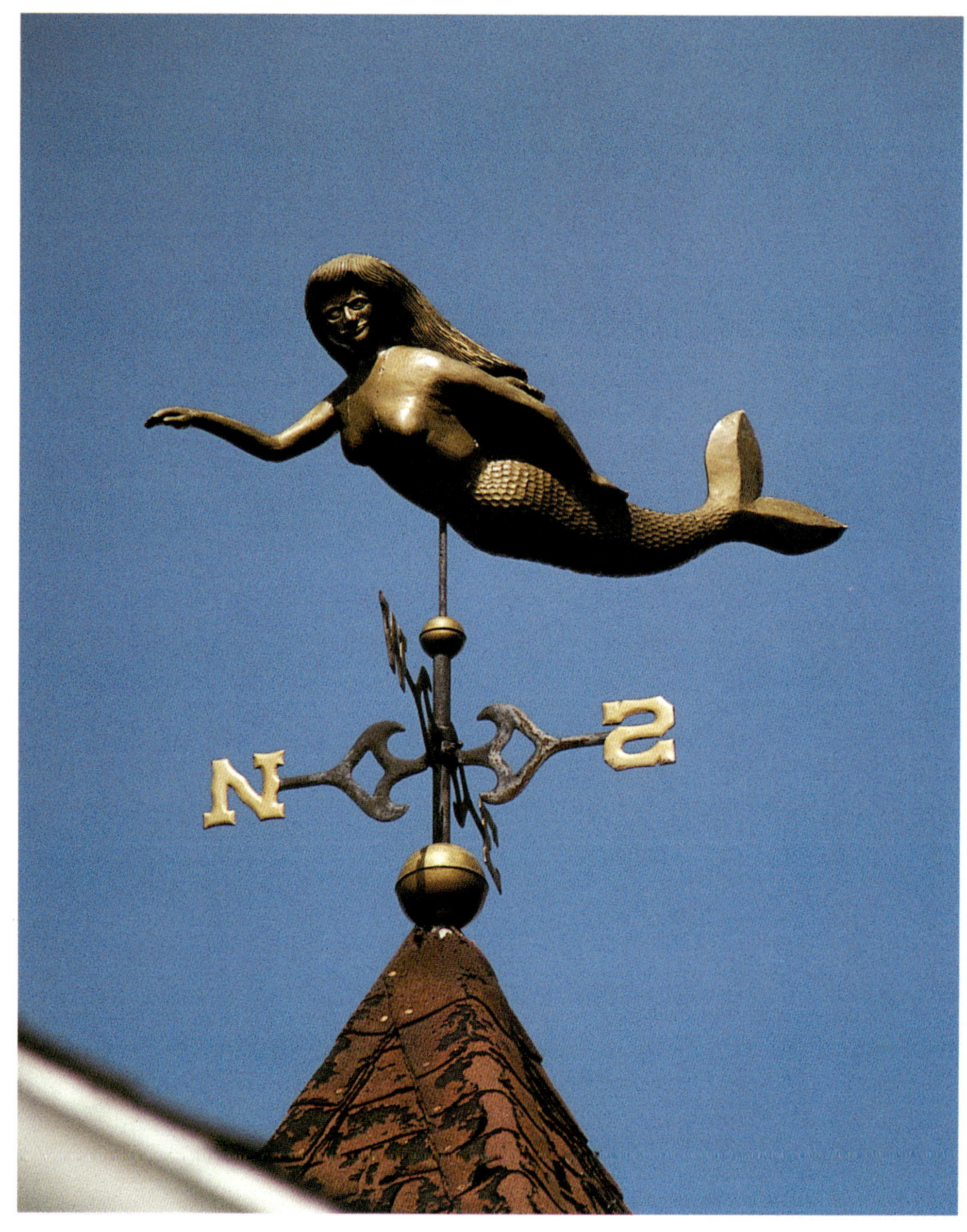

This delicate silhouette of the angel Gabriel is an exact replica of an old one. The horn has been broken at the mouth.

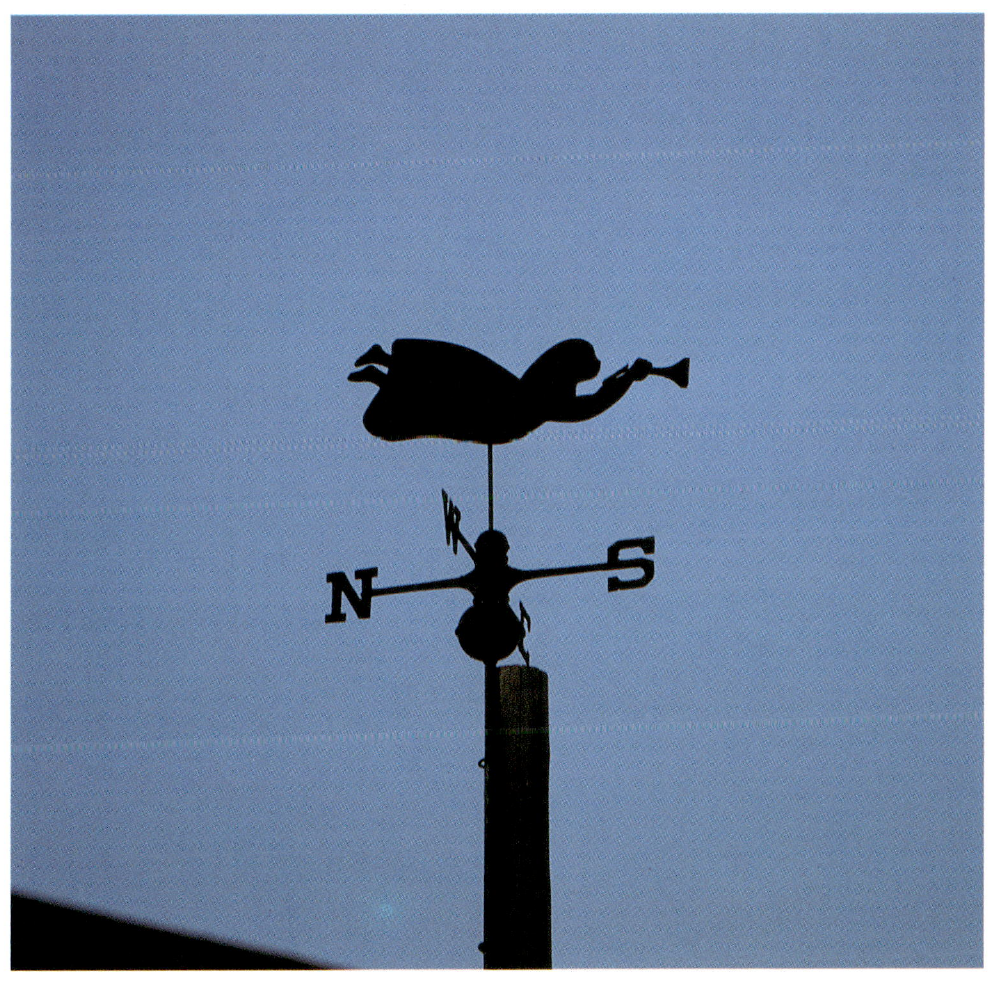

This lovely sheet-iron silhouette of the angel Gabriel was found in Kennebec County. It is from the late nineteenth century. Courtesy of Kenneth and Ida Manko

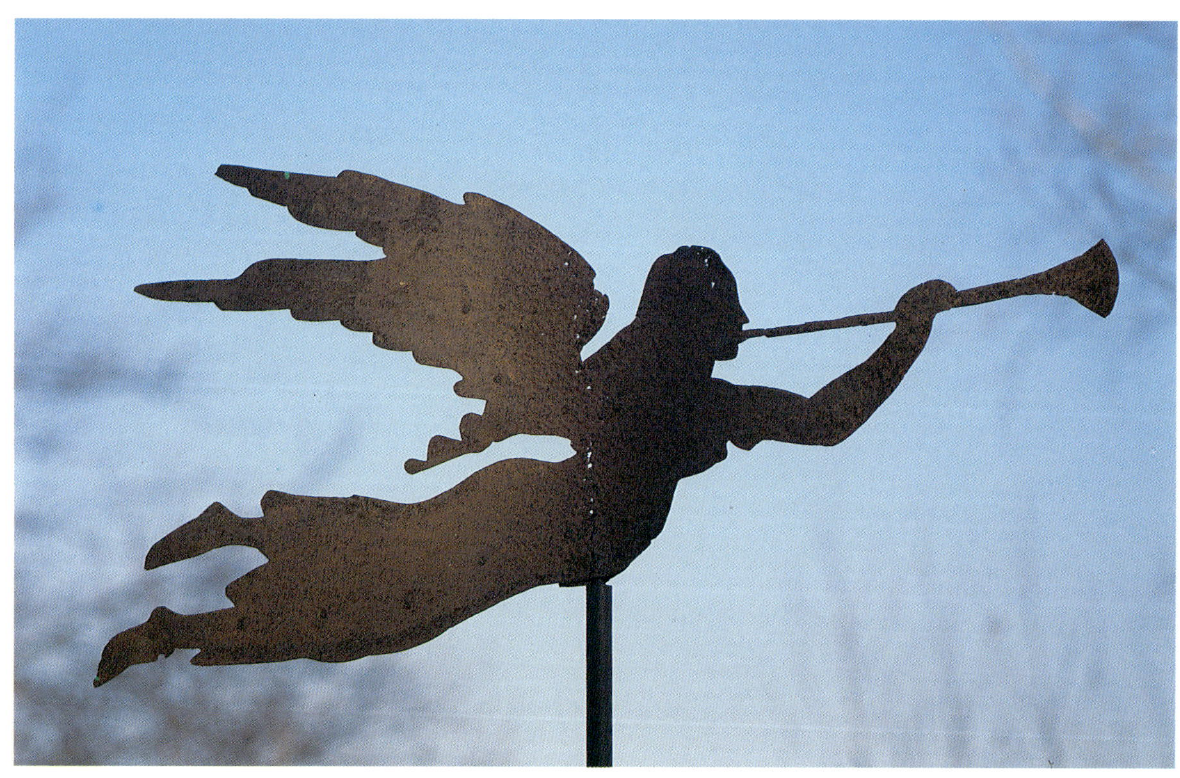

High Street Congregational Church, in Auburn, is topped by a phoenix, the magical bird of Greek mythology. According to legend, only one such bird existed at a time. When the bird reached the end of its life cycle, somewhere between 500 and 12,954 years, it would burn itself on a funeral pyre, and a new, beautiful bird would then rise from the ashes. It has become a symbol of immortality and spiritual rebirth.

Like the phoenix, the Auburn church was destroyed by fire in 1985. When the new church was rebuilt, one of the members came up with the idea of putting a phoenix vane on the new building, and the congregation commissioned this elegant new vane from William McElvain, of Searsport.

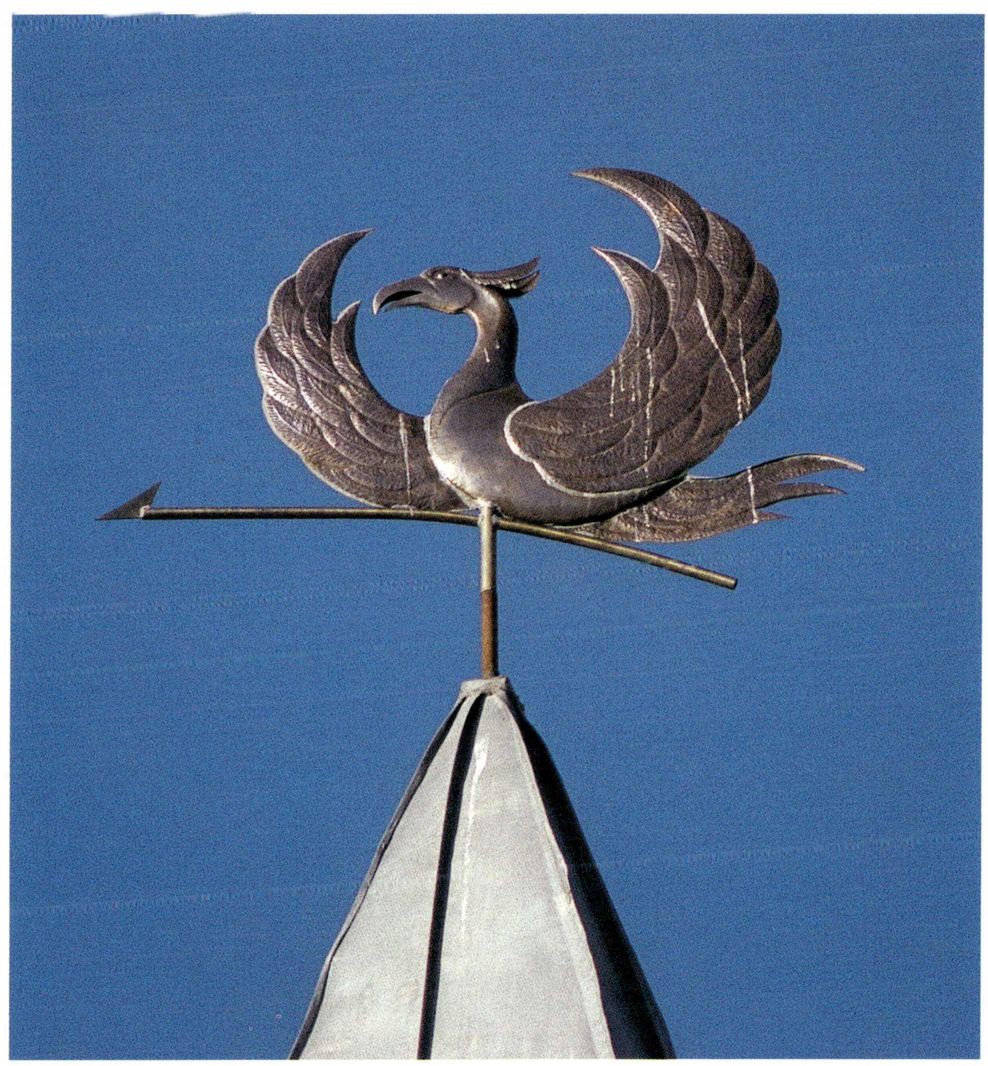

A beautiful sky provided the perfect backdrop for this elegantly simple split banner atop what is now the American Legion building in Bath. It was originally a Methodist Church built in the 1850s. The belfry was added in 1858, and presumably the vane was put on then.

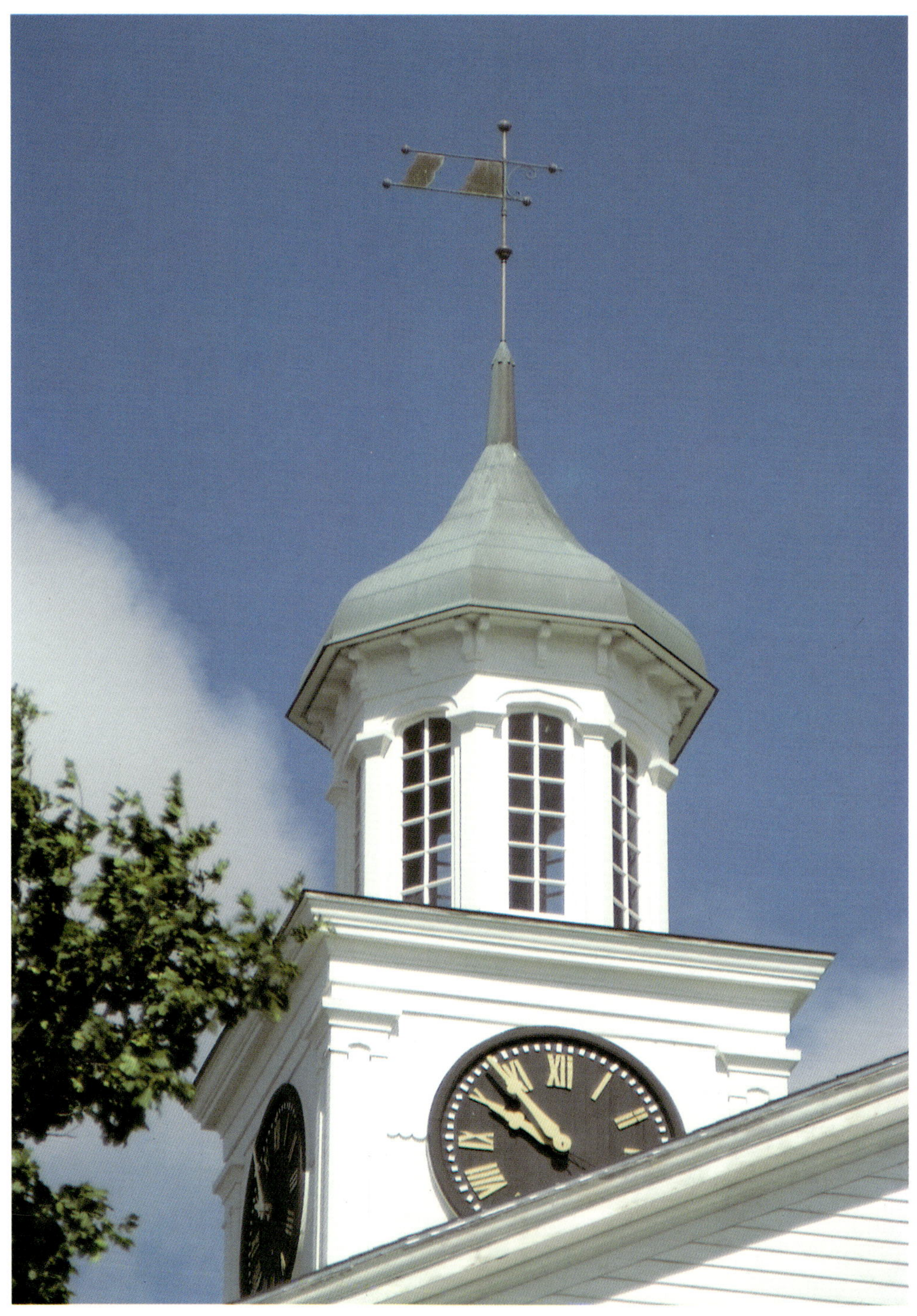

Scrolls and Banners

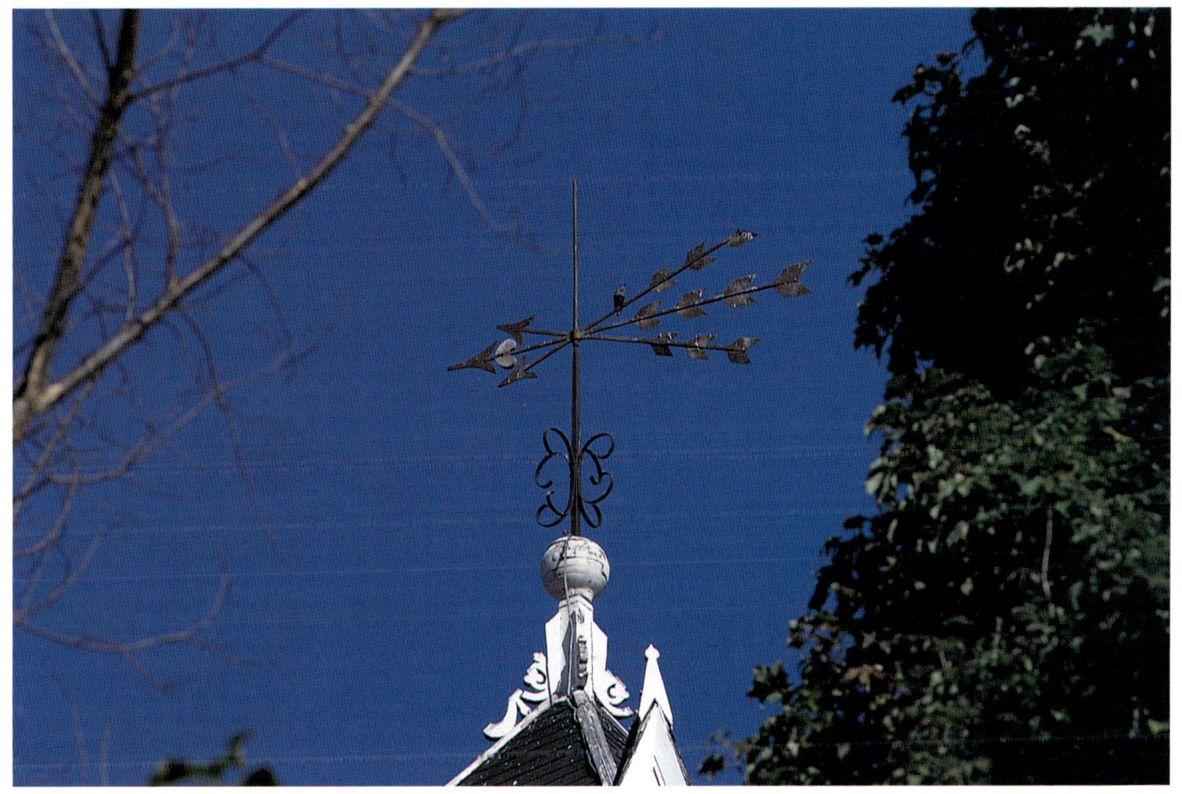

Preceding page: *A delicate and effective arrangement of arrows is seen in this lovely vane on the United Methodist Church of West Baldwin. The middle arrow pierces a heart. It dates from 1860 to 1880.*

A Roman scroll design has a heavier look than the more traditional classical scrolls. The highly stylized lines of this vane offer a bold look. It appears to be from the 1920s and is on the Poland Community Church.

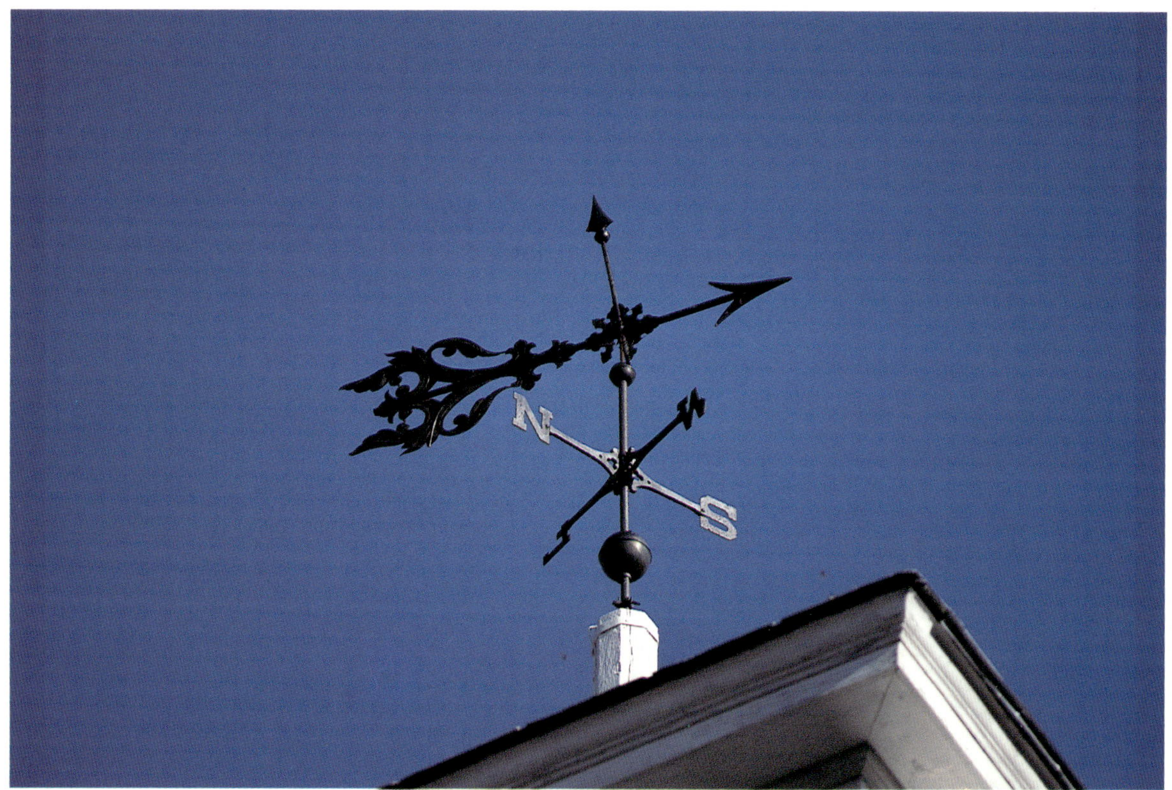

The lovely swallowtail banner on the First Parish Church of Portland is said to be Maine's oldest vane still in use. It was made in 1760 by Thomas Drowne, a relative of the most famous weather vane maker of them all, Deacon Shem Drowne. This vane originally sat on a previous meeting house and was moved to the present church after it was built in 1825.

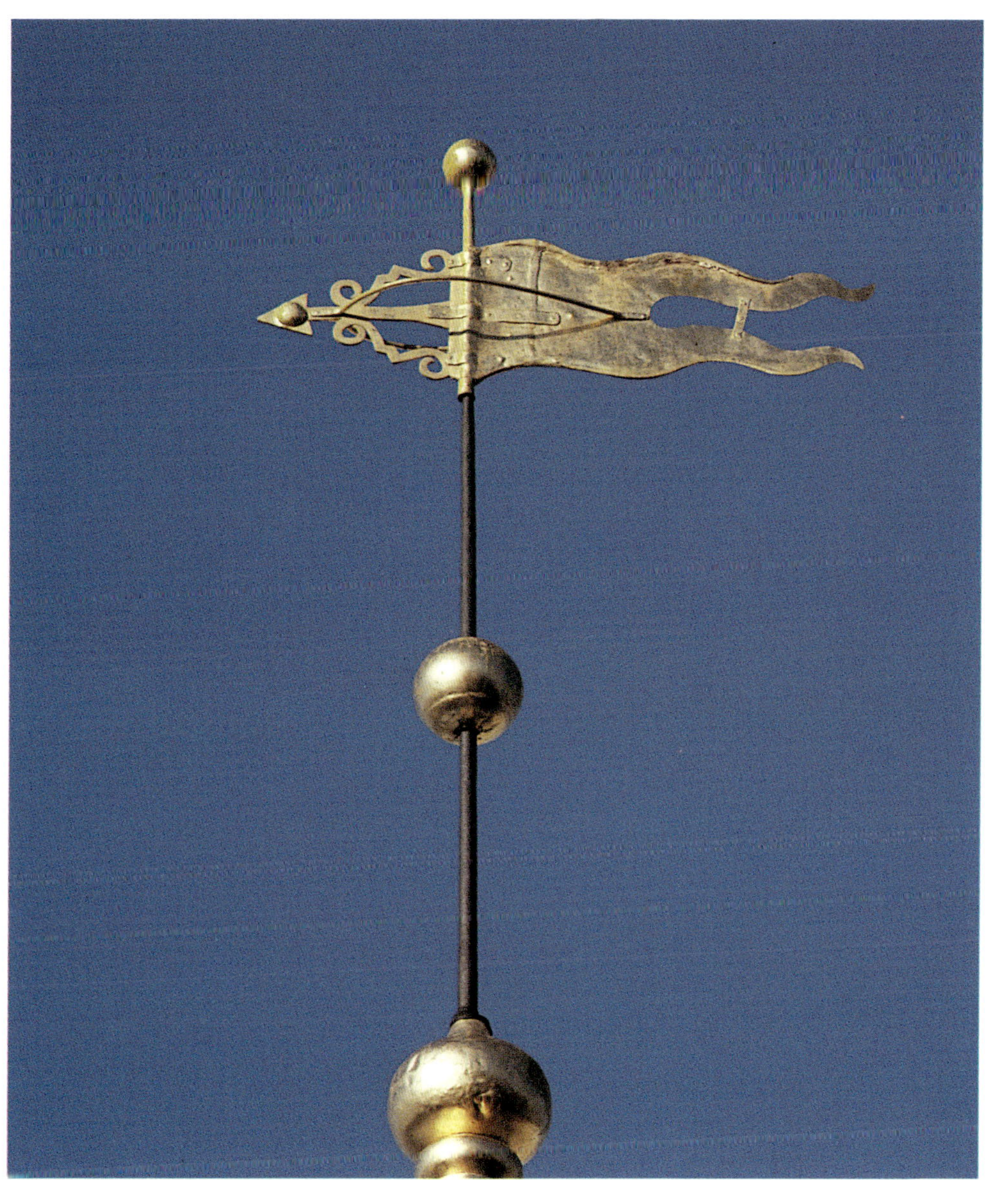

The South Congregational Church in Kennebunkport displays this old wooden banneret. The church was built in 1824, although the vane was not added until the latter part of the nineteenth century. It was made by Lewis Martin.

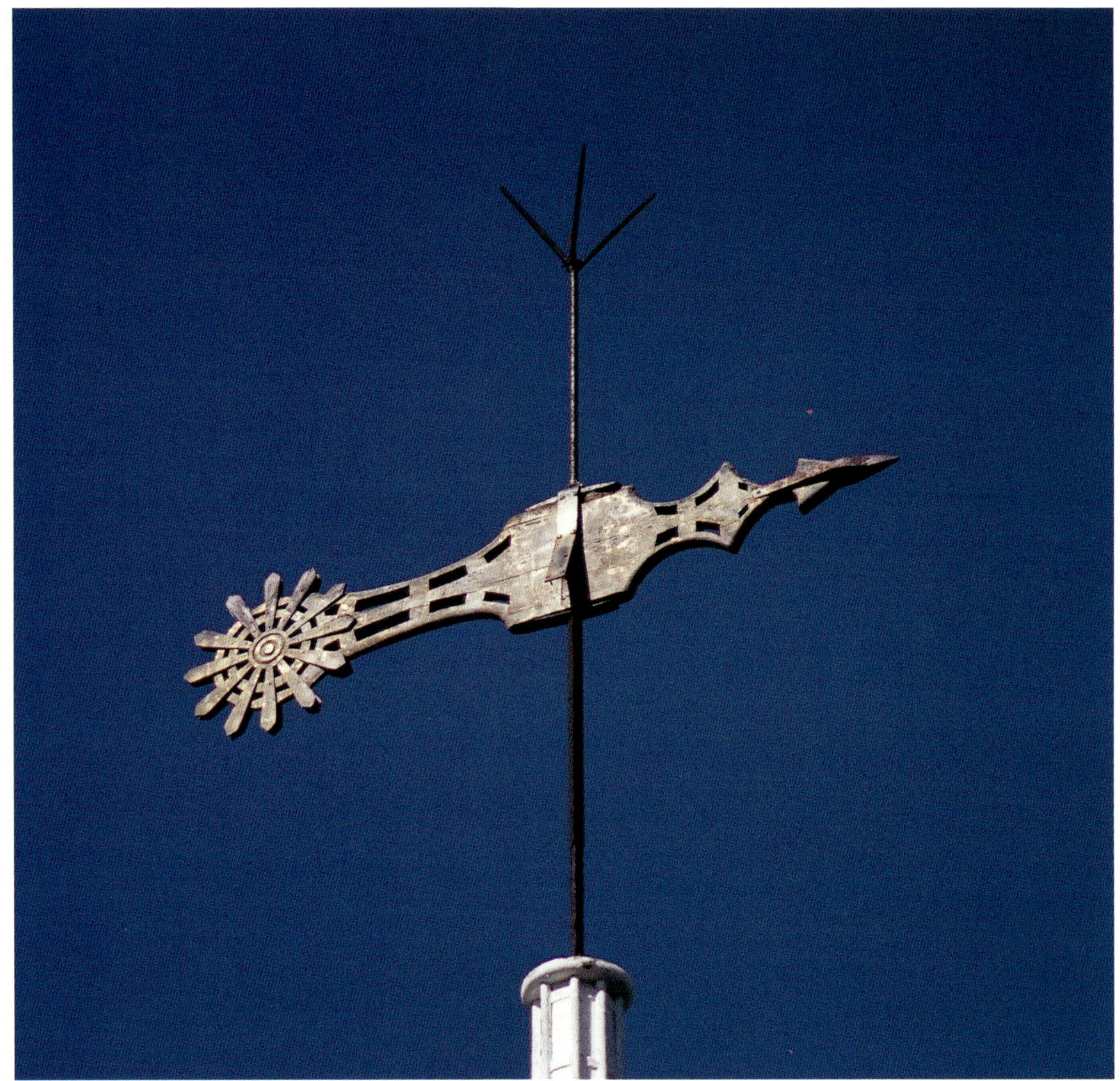

The date and location of this banneret are worked into its design. A face is visible in the sun motif, the point is made from a star, and two more stars complete the swallowtail. The solid circle connected to the sun may represent a full moon. Tory Hill is near Buxton. The first pastor of the church, the Reverend Paul Coffin, came to Buxton in the early eighteenth century, and as he and many of his parishioners were Royalists, that area became known as Tory Hill.

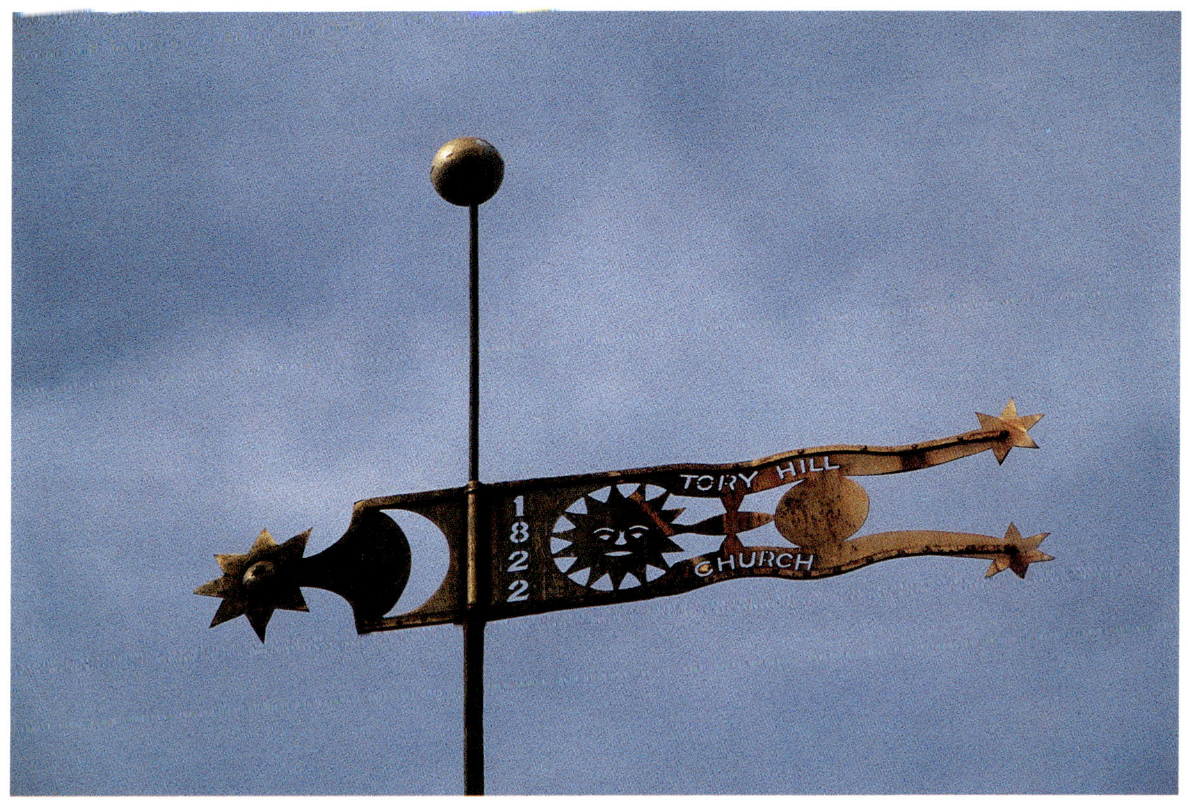

This striking, bold banner on the York County Courthouse was erected in 1854. It was one of the few things to survive a 1933 fire that destroyed the entire central section of the building. When the courthouse was rebuilt, the weather vane was rehung.

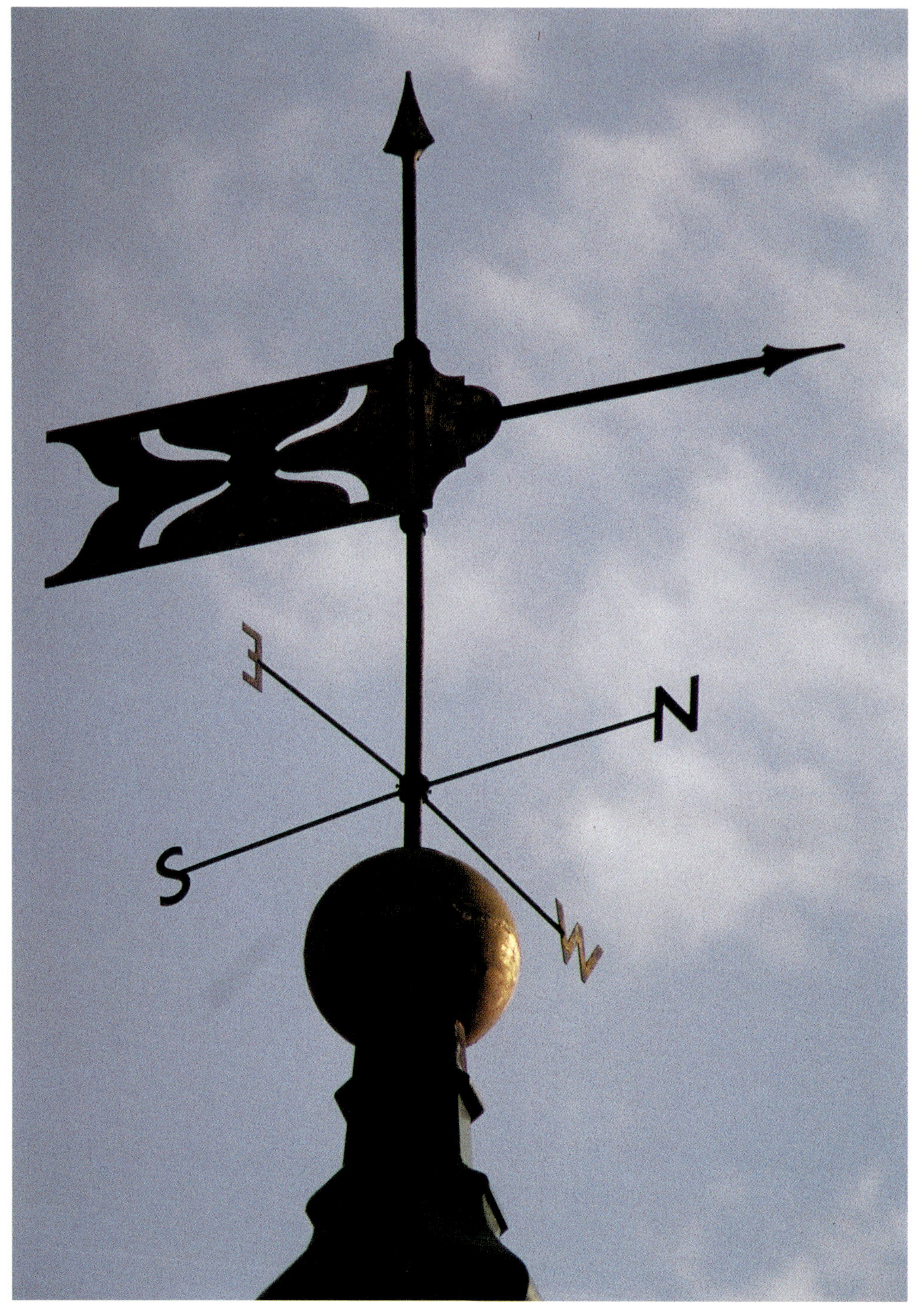

Informed sources believe that this copper banner is a replacement. The original was on the Wesley Street Methodist Church in Bath, which burned to the ground in 1898. The congregation immediately rebuilt, and dedicated their new church on July 22, 1899. A photograph taken of the church in that month shows the weather vane and cardinals already in place on the steeple. During the 1960s, the congregation moved to the Methodist Church building on North Washington Street in Bath, taking the vane with them. A decade later that building was sold to Bath Iron Works, which still owns it. Traces of either gold leaf or old yellow paint still show on the old vane.

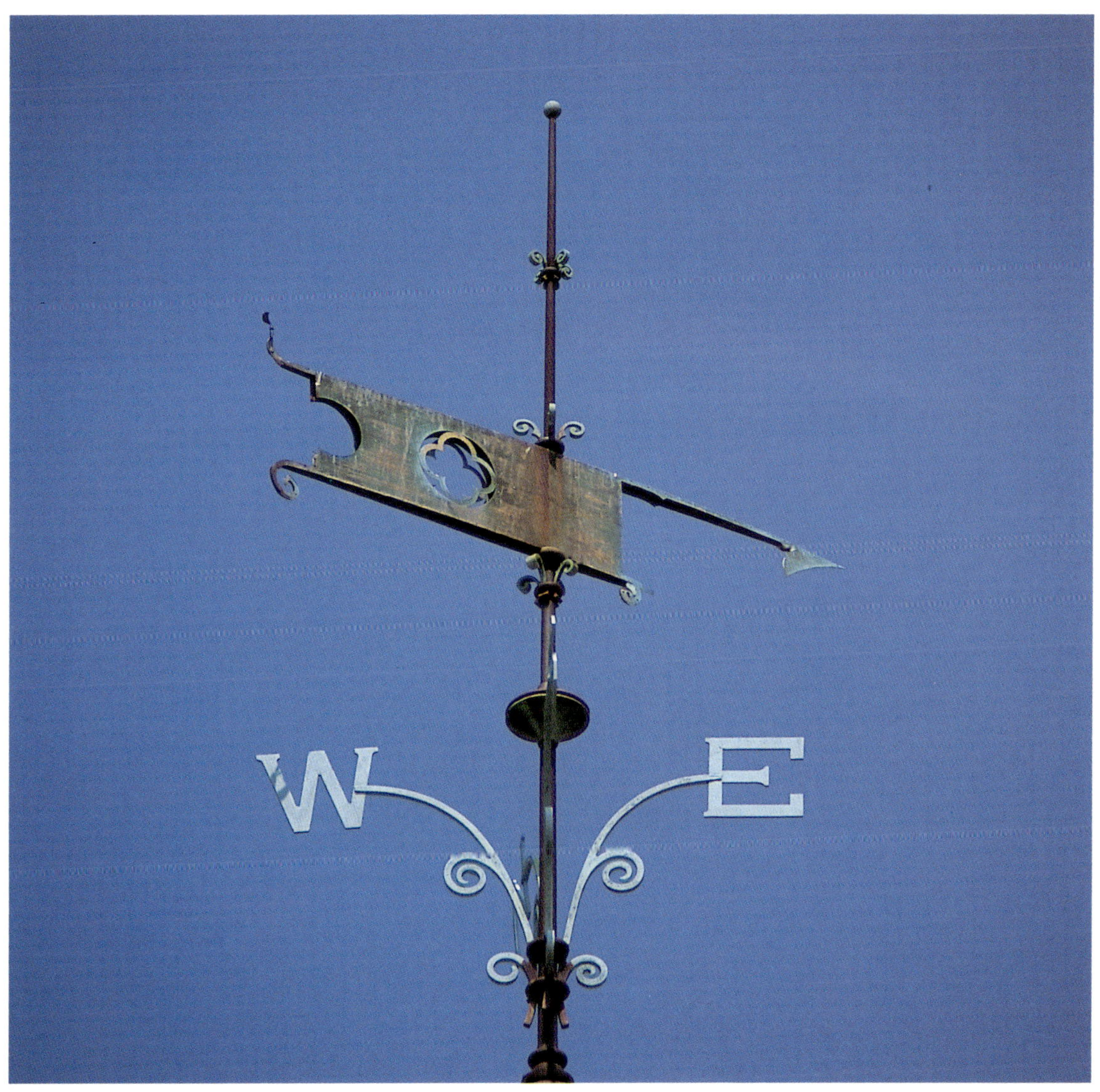

It is unusual to see an 1880s-style lyre painted silver. This leads to speculation that it was repainted in the 1930s, when silver paint was commonly used in place of expensive gold leaf.

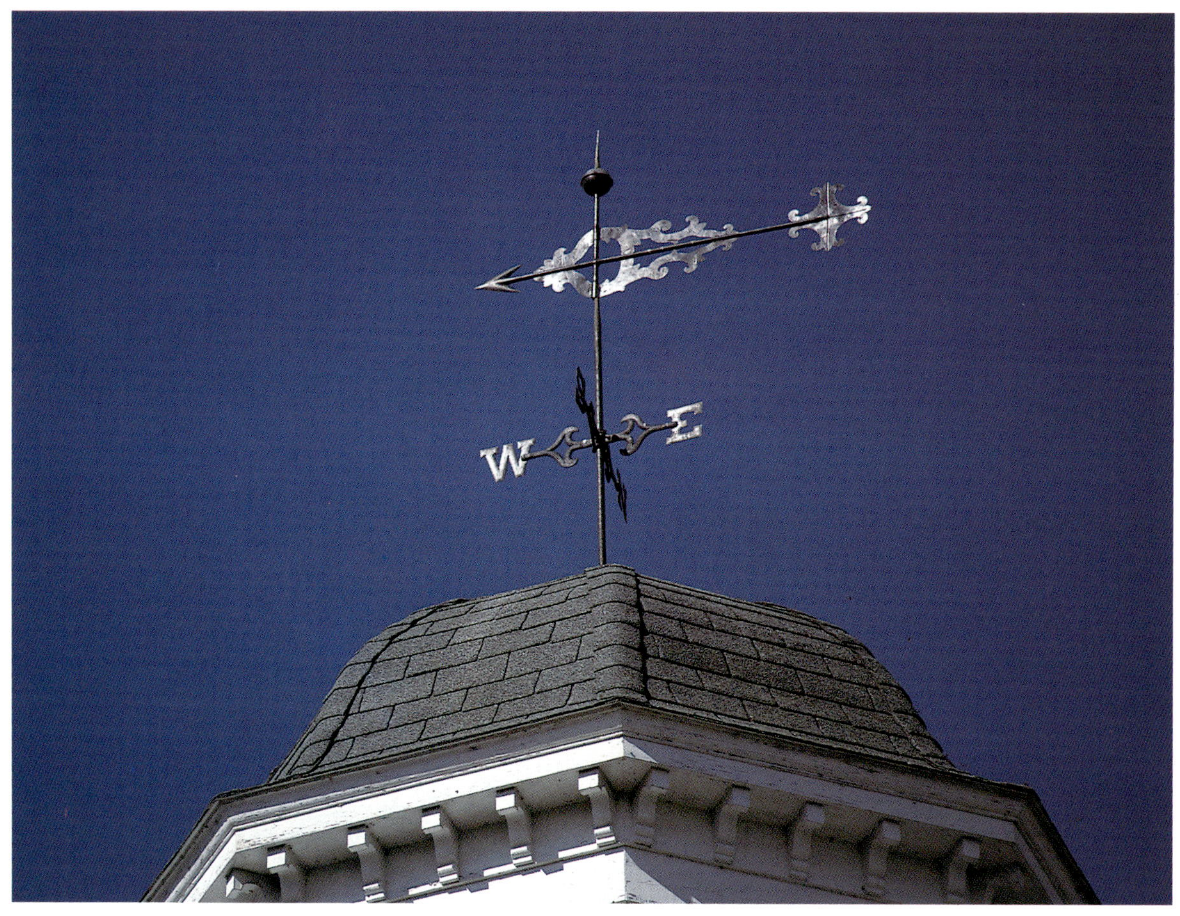

This turn-of-the-century banneret sits on top of the Old Carriage House in Bath, the only building left on the historic site formerly occupied by the Hotel Sedgwick, the Erudition School, North Church, and Shaw's Mansion. A medical center has taken over the site and is now preserving this part of Bath's history.

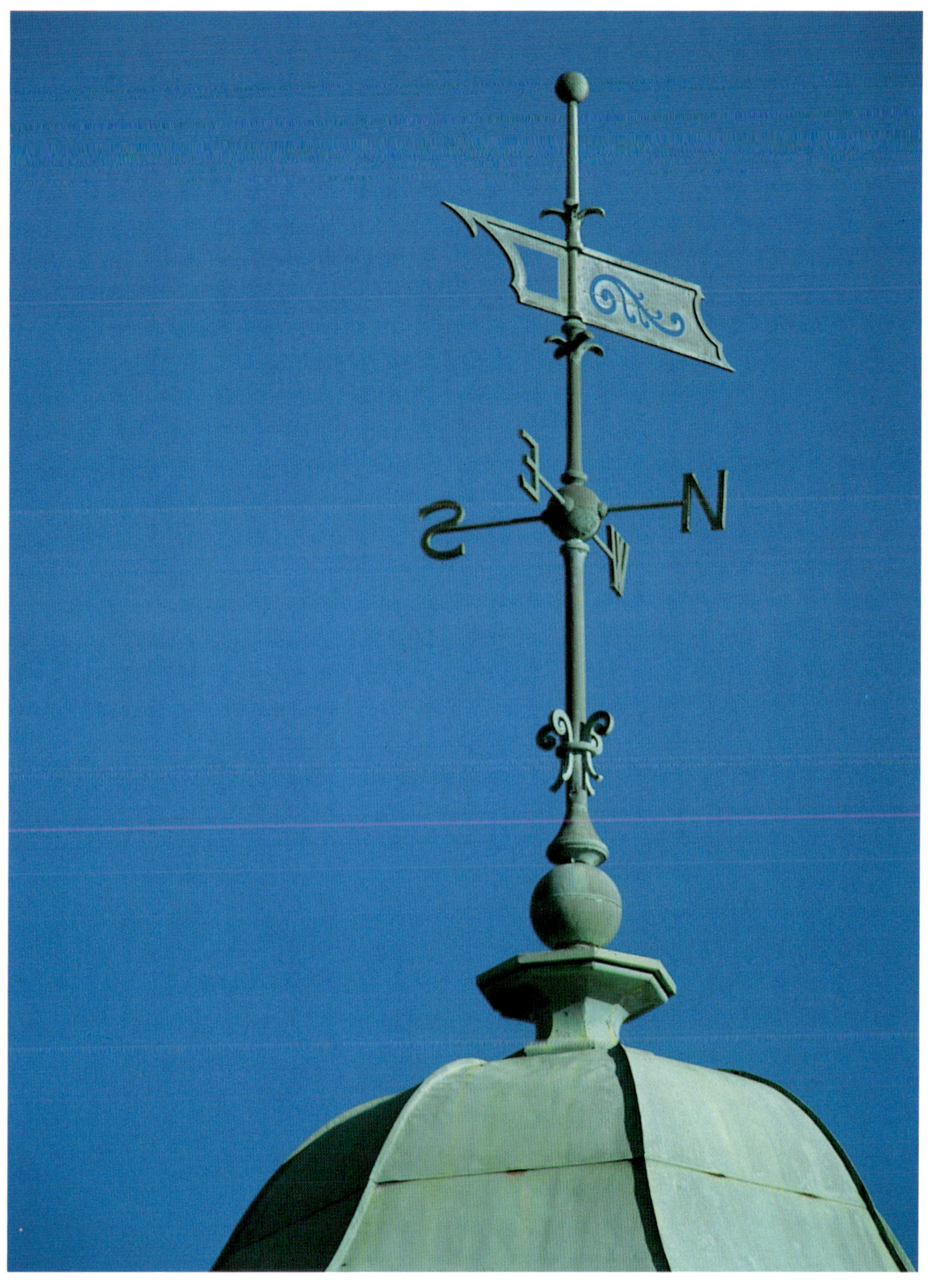

The Head Tide Meeting House is topped by a bold arrow. It is an exact copy of the original vane, which was destroyed with the steeple in a 1962 fire. The straight lines of this arrow contrast sharply to the more intricate designs of the scroll weathervanes.

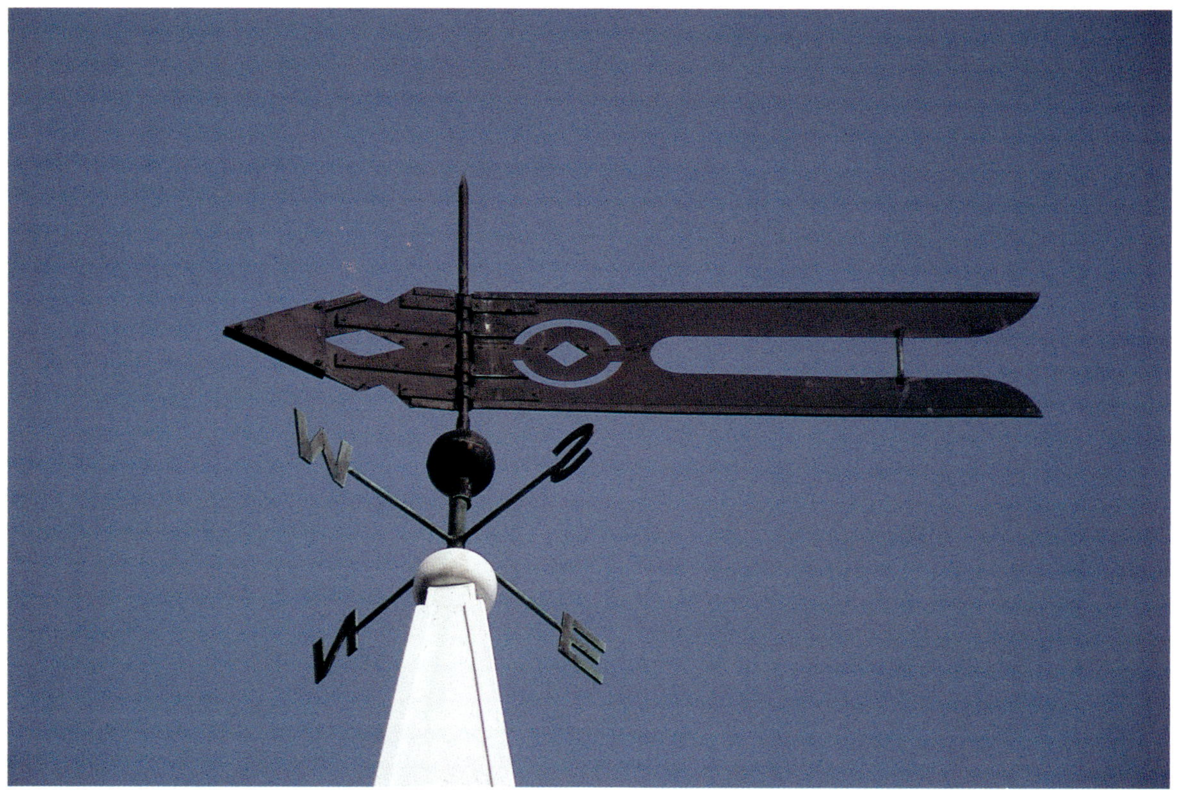

A beautifully designed old banneret provides the topping for one of only two round steeples in the state of Maine. The vane sits on Yarmouth's Old Baptist Meeting House, which was built in 1796. Since 1889, the former meeting house has been Memorial Hall for the Town of Yarmouth.

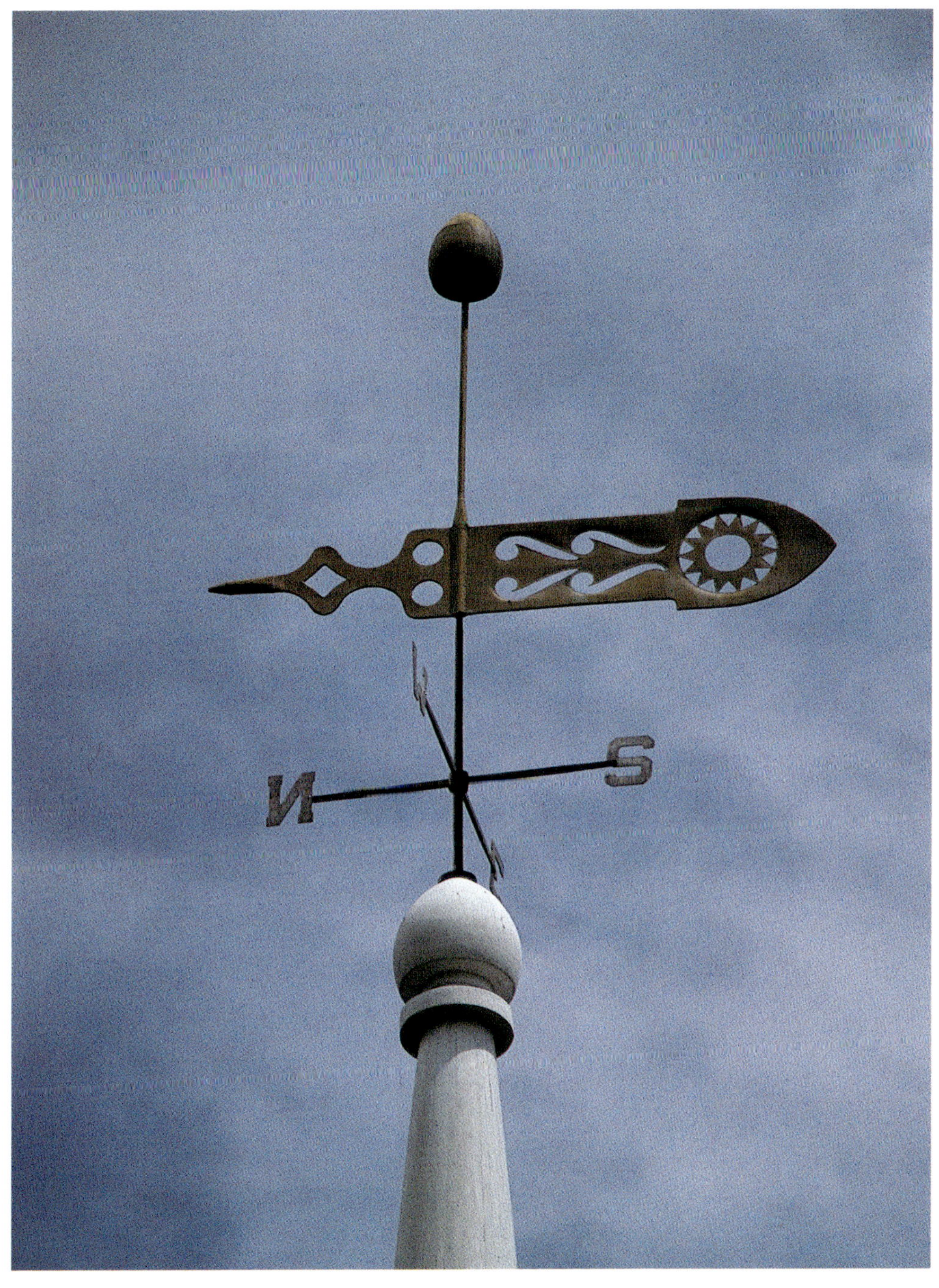

Several sunflowers complement this Gothic-revival flag thought to date from between 1870 and 1880.

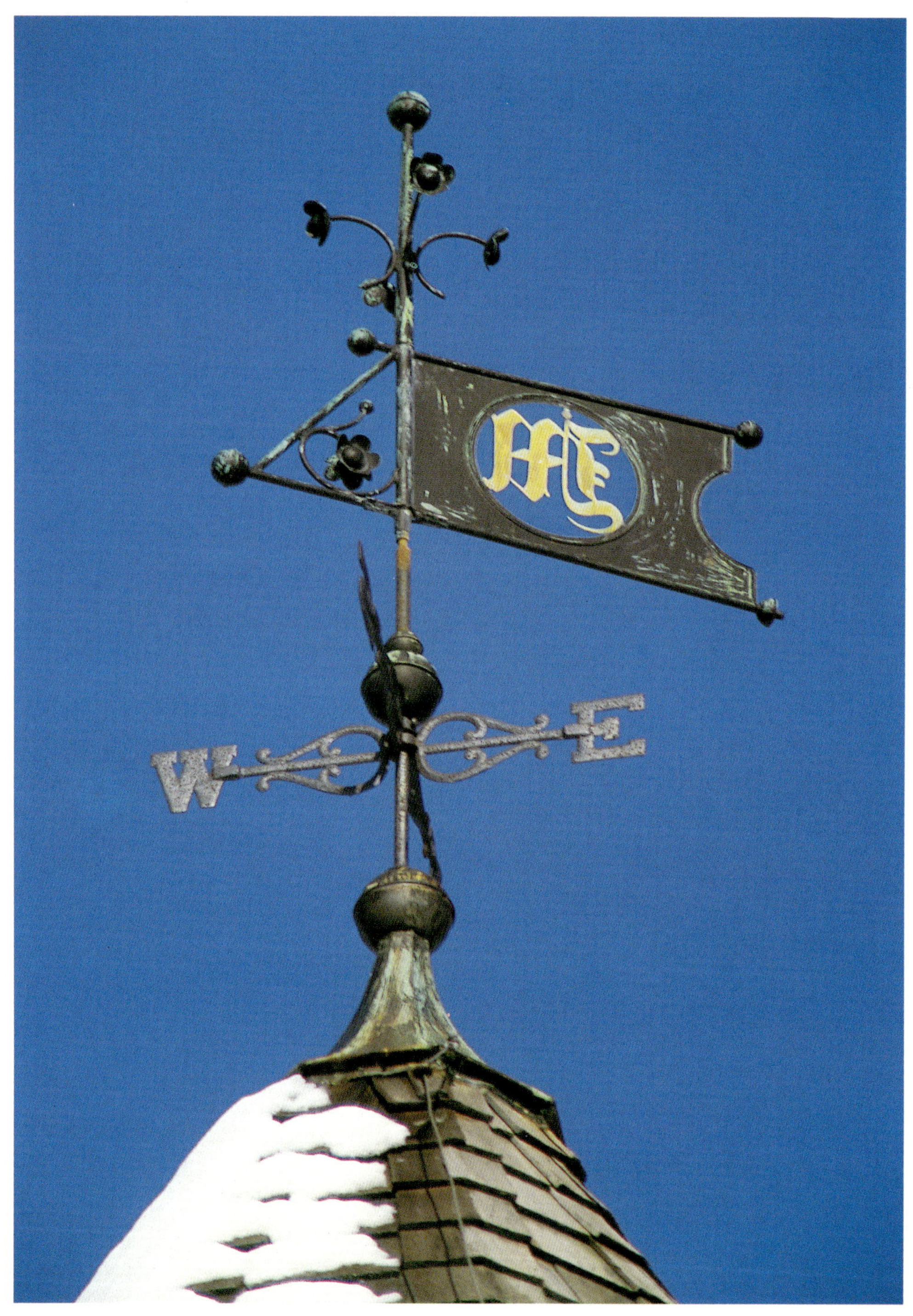

On the turret of the Skowhegan Free Public Library sits the original weather vane, dated 1889. Cut-out details in the banner are more than just ornamental. The shamrock design in the center of the Gothic-revival flag is also a repeated design on the upper front part of the library, which houses a special Memorial Room for Civil War. The shamrock was a symbol for a military organization of the time. The flag appears to be copper and is in excellent condition.

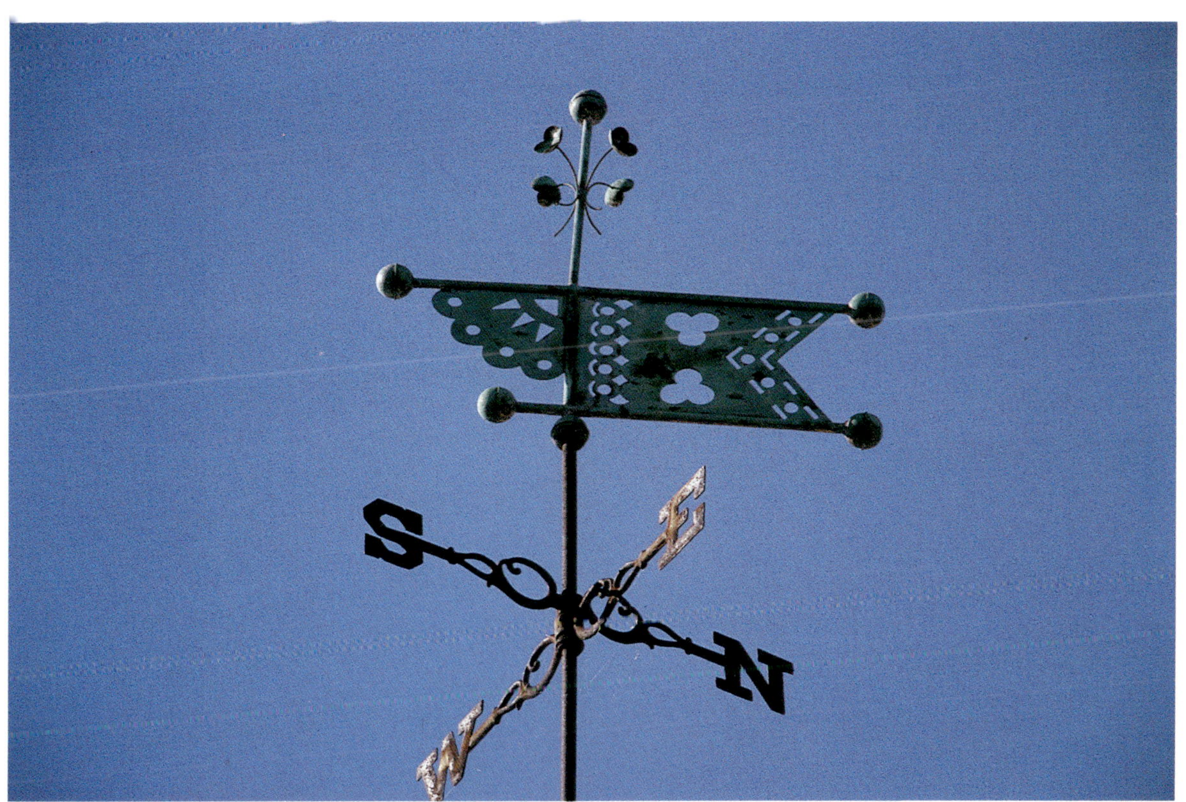

This 1800s lyre has not only stayed on the same house through the years, but has stayed in the same family. The center is black, while the arrow, tail, balls, and cardinals are painted yellow.

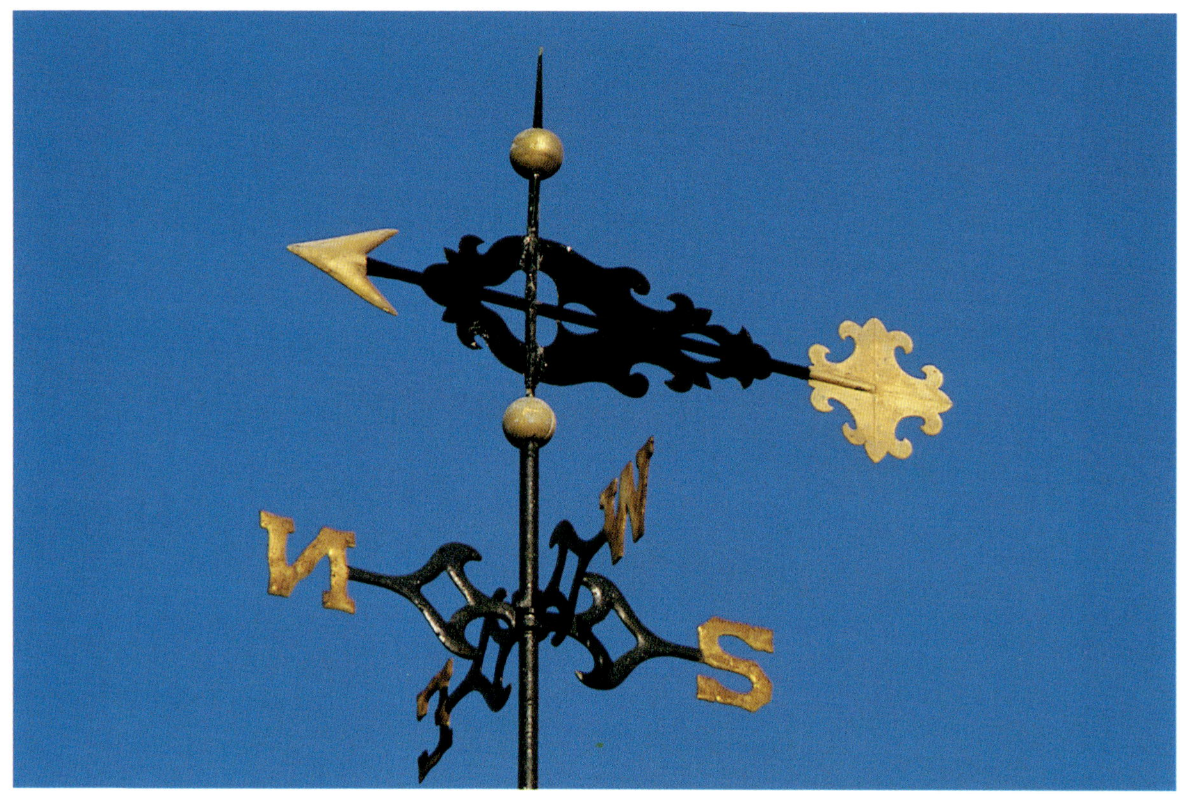

Sunshine gleams from this 1880s Gothic-revival flag. It is made of copper covered with gold leaf.

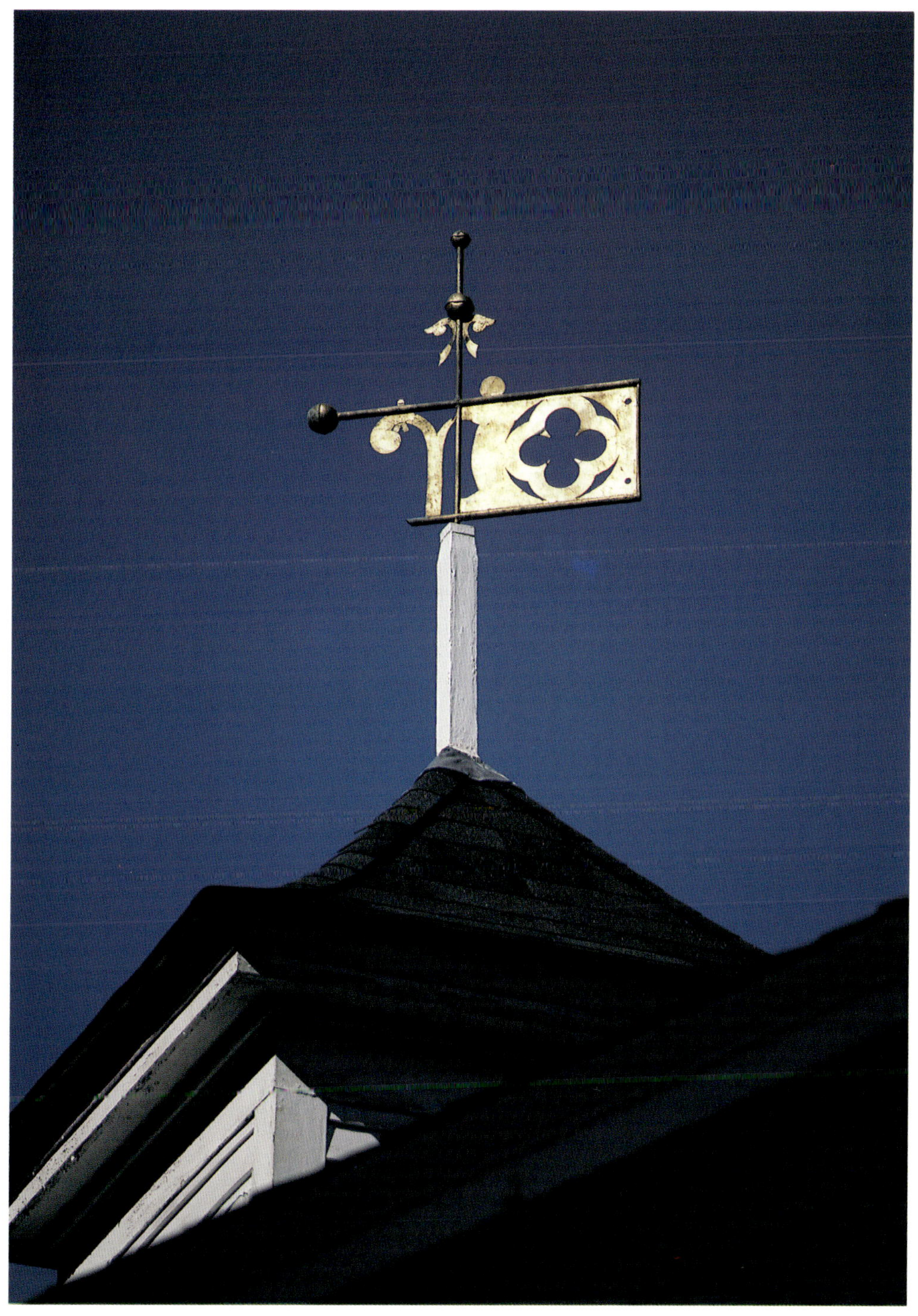

This weather vane–lightning rod has a distinctive style. It dates back to the early 1900s, possibly earlier.

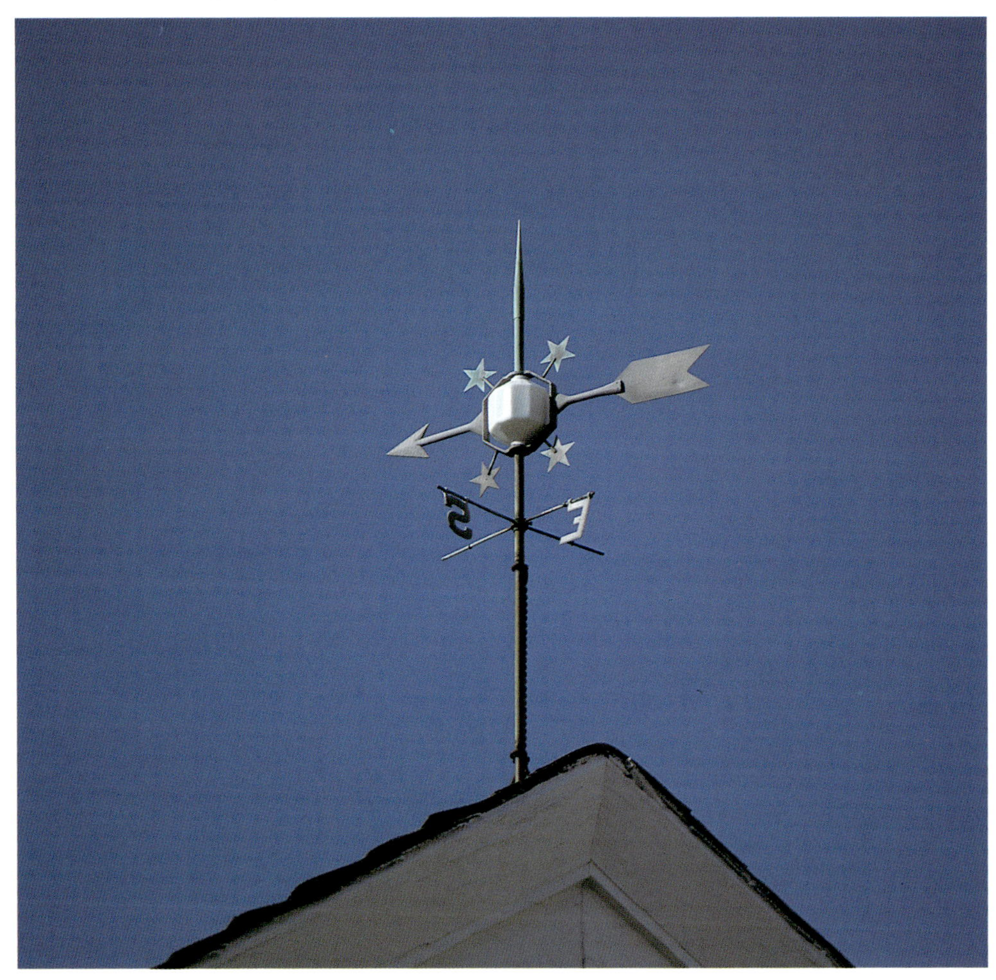

A delicate old scroll dating back to the 1860s appears to be in good condition even though its cardinals are broken. It is on an old church in Oxford which has been converted to an antiques shop.

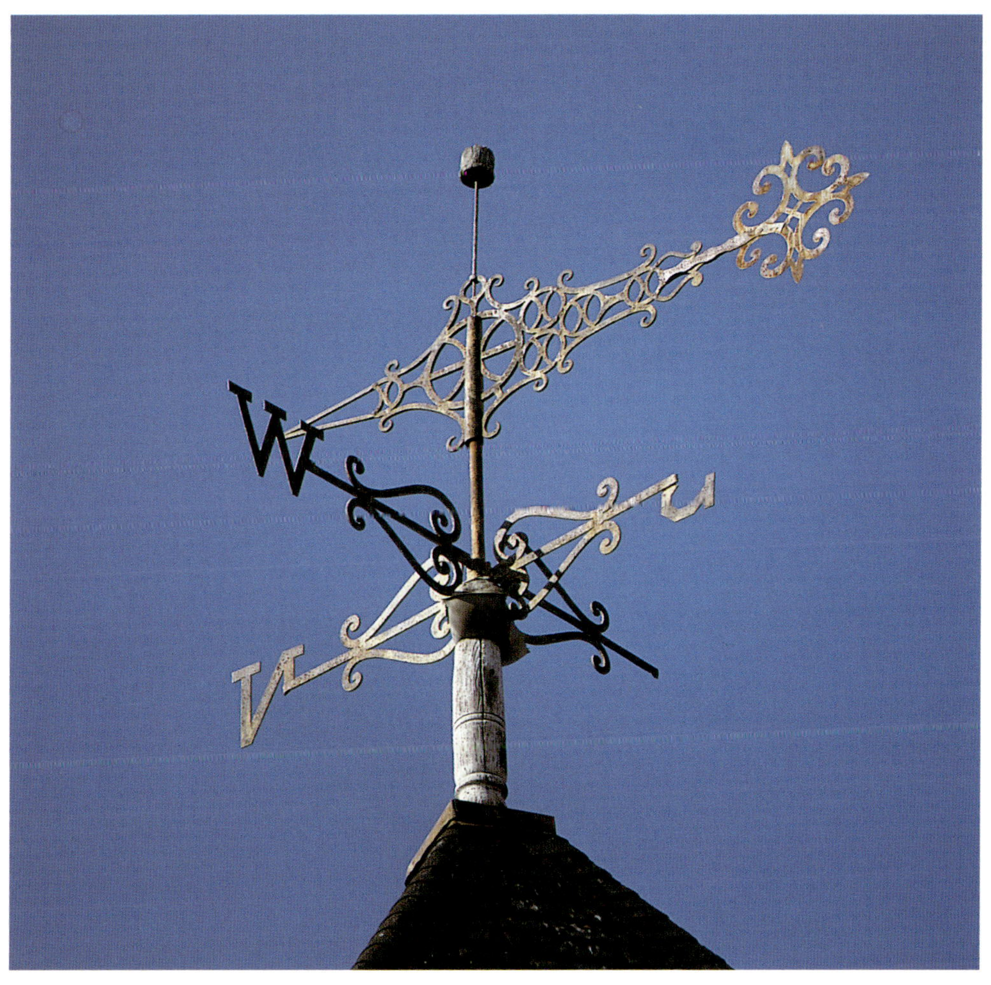

Most lyres appear on churches, but this one sits atop a mid-1800s barn. The decorative classical lines are typical of nineteenth-century lyres.

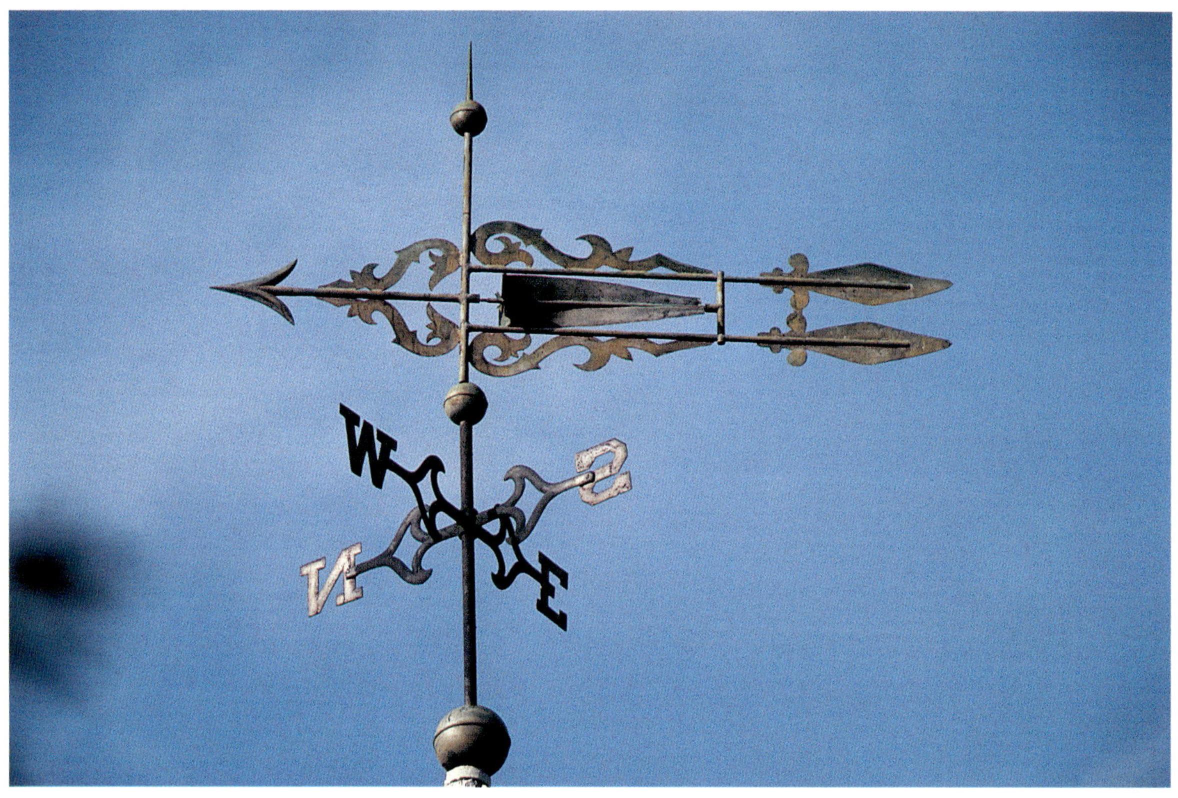

This banneret holds special meaning for me. It is the old original vane from the steeple of the Elijah Kellogg Church on Harpswell, the church I attend when in Maine. Now it is in the home of a church member. It dates back to the mid 1800s, is made of wood, and still has traces of gold leaf on its surface. Its original purpose was more than merely decorative. As Elijah Kellogg, the pastor of this church in the mid 1800s, so eloquently wrote:

Its spire shall be the last to meet,
The parting seaman's lingering eye,
The first his homeward step to greet,
And point him to a home on high

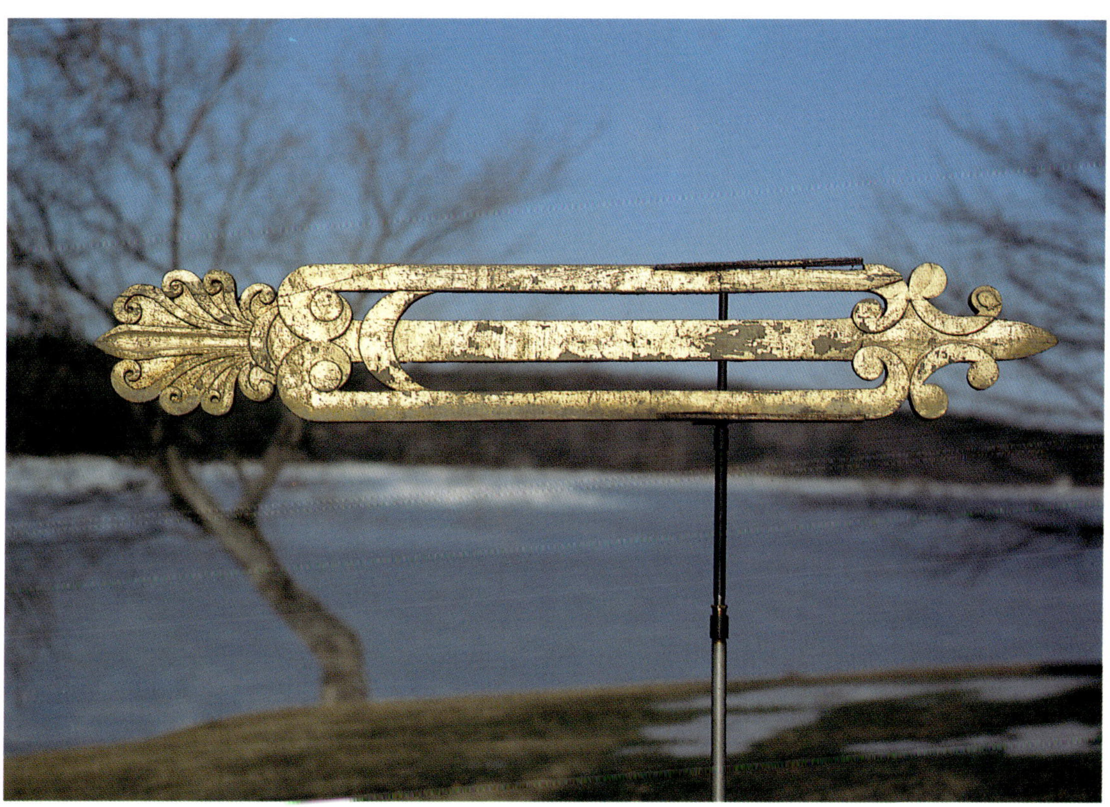

A simple silhouette conveys the close ties and single purpose of a hunter and his dogs. This vane is crafted from iron.

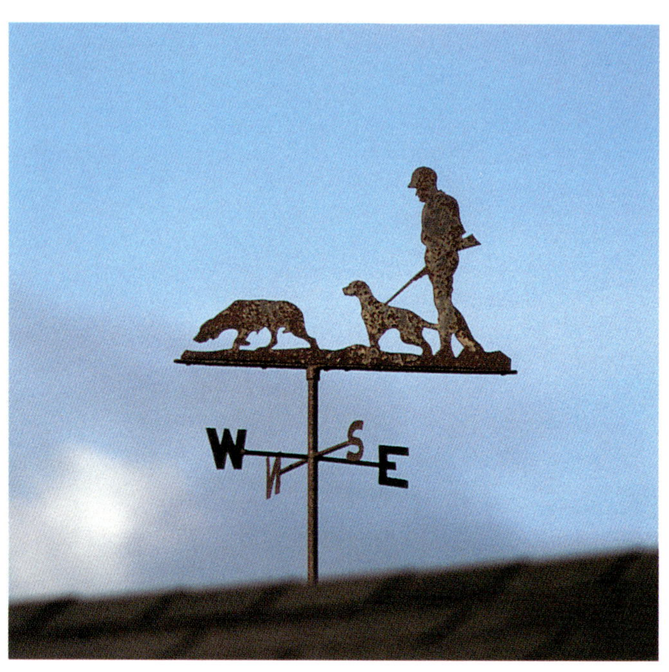

Facing page: *This choice Massasoit Indian Chief vane came from Penobscot County. Gold leaf covers the copper. It dates from between 1900 and 1930.* Courtesy of Kenneth and Ida Manko

Human Endeavors

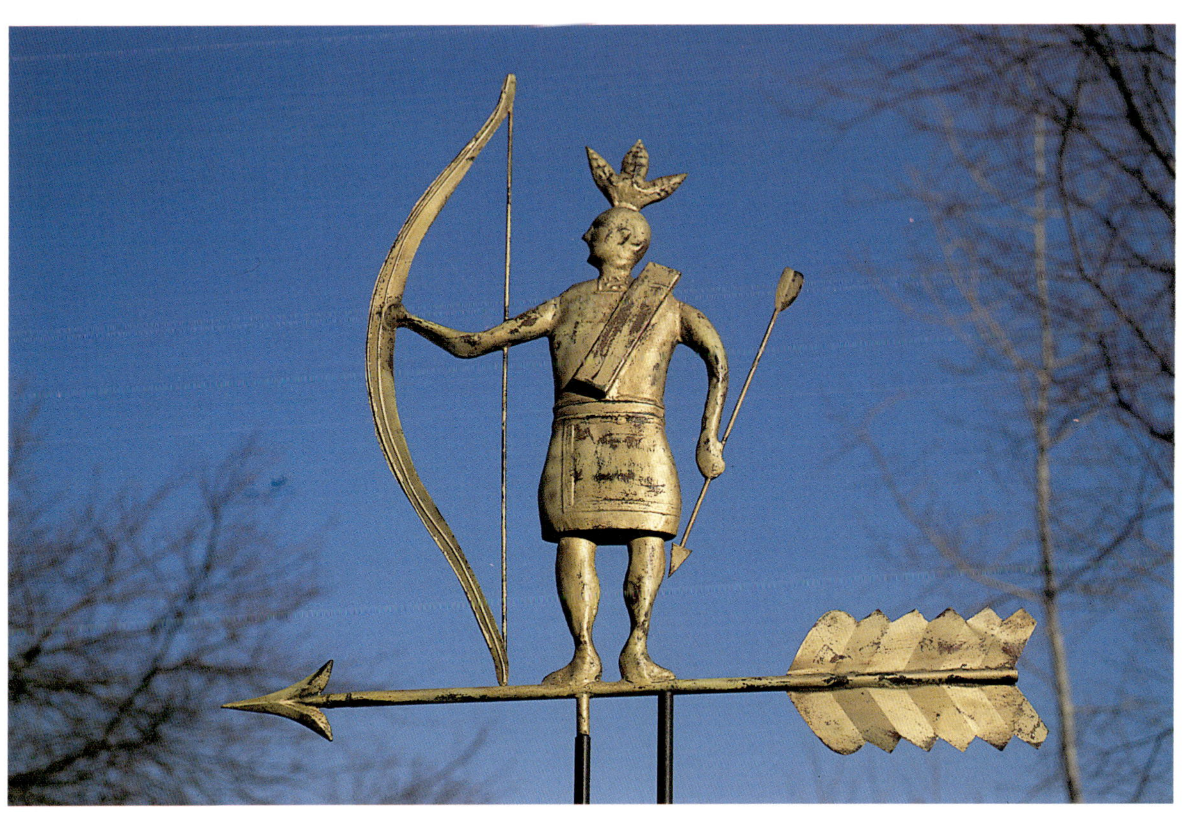

The portly peg-legged gentleman looking through the spy glass is Peter Stuyvesant (1592–1672), the last Dutch governor of the colony of New Netherland (New York). This special vane is from the early 1800s. When the owners sold their previous home (with Governor Stuyvesant on the rooftop), they missed the vane so much that they arranged with the new owners to get it back in exchange for a microwave oven.

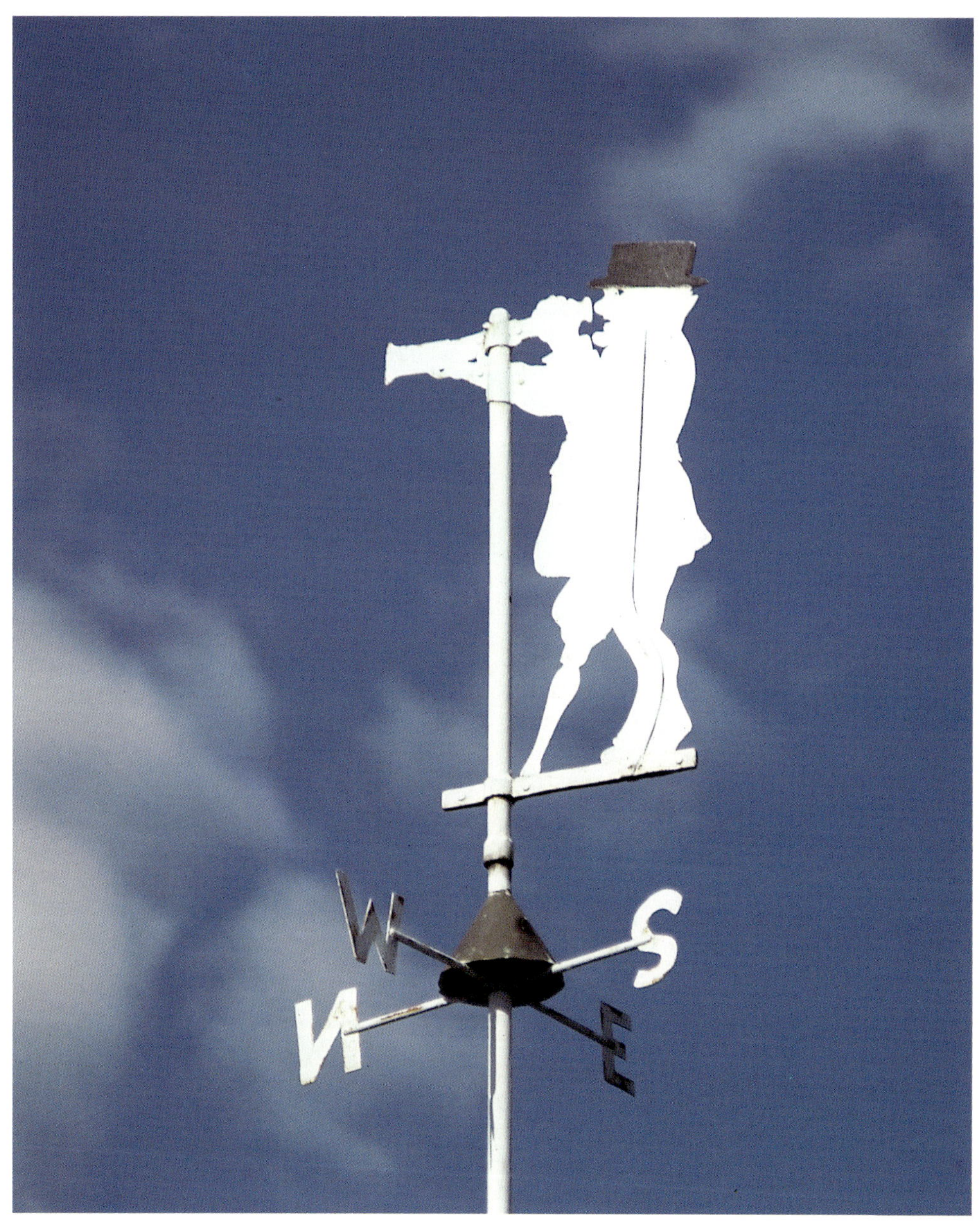

A unique handcrafted Indian paddling a canoe provides a striking contrast to the deep blue sky. This twentieth-century painted tin vane was made by the owner's uncle. The strong, determined profile conveys a sense of power and courage.

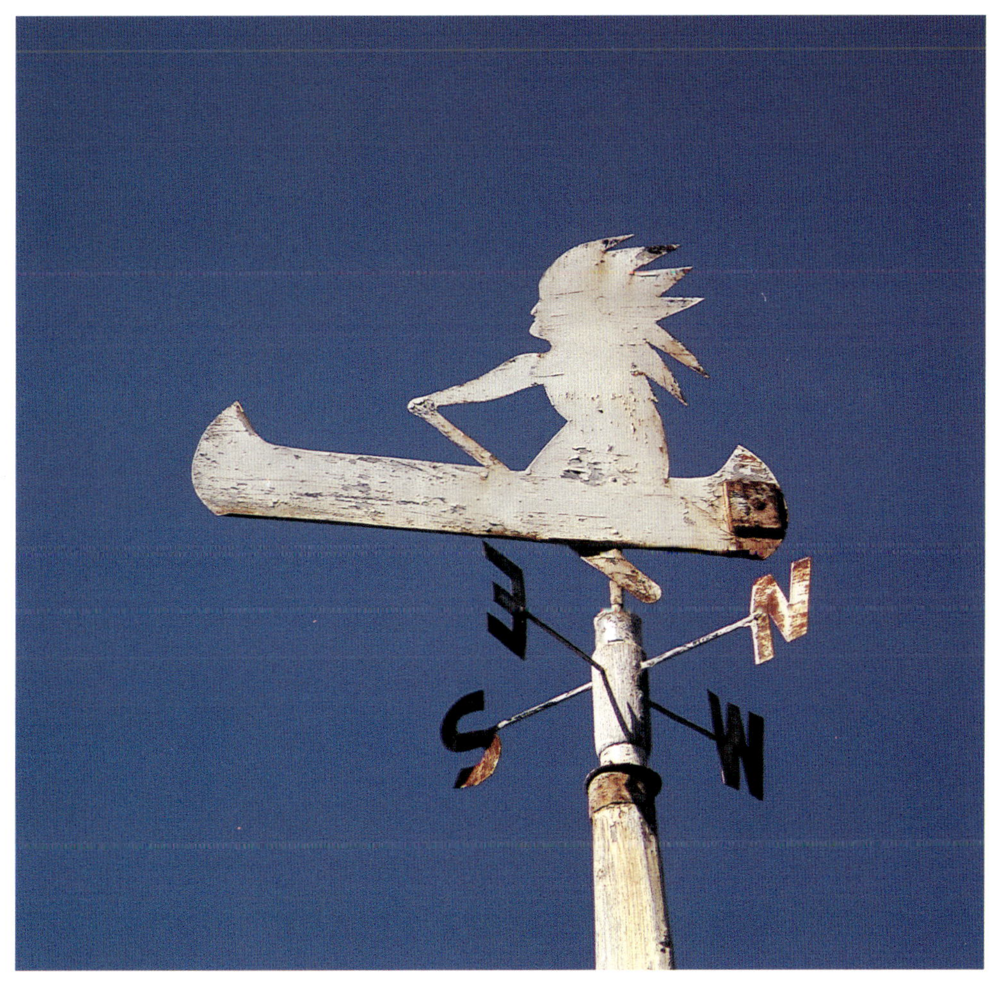

This new copper train was made by craftsman William McElvain, who also crafted the phoenix vane shown earlier. Careful attention to detail is evident in this piece.

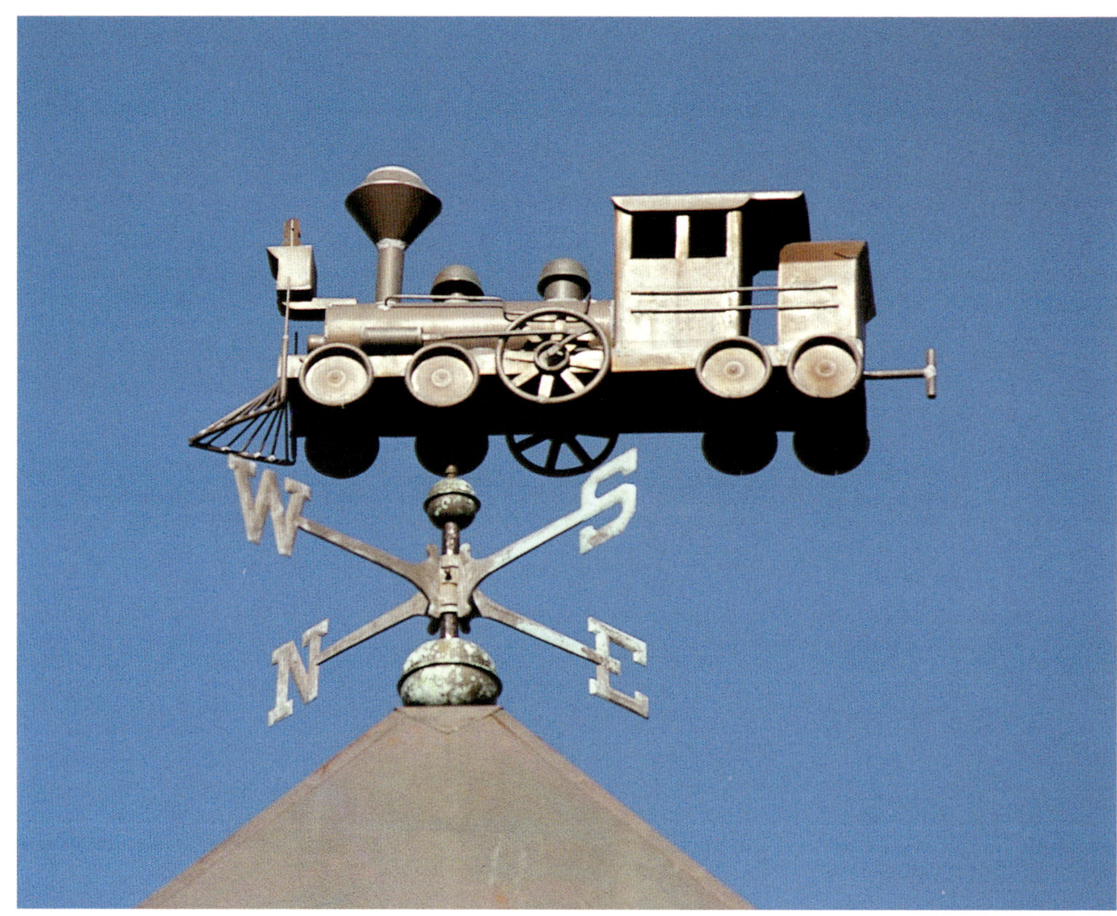

An old model airplane obviously indicates a twentieth-century theme. The realistic engine holds a propeller that turns with the wind.

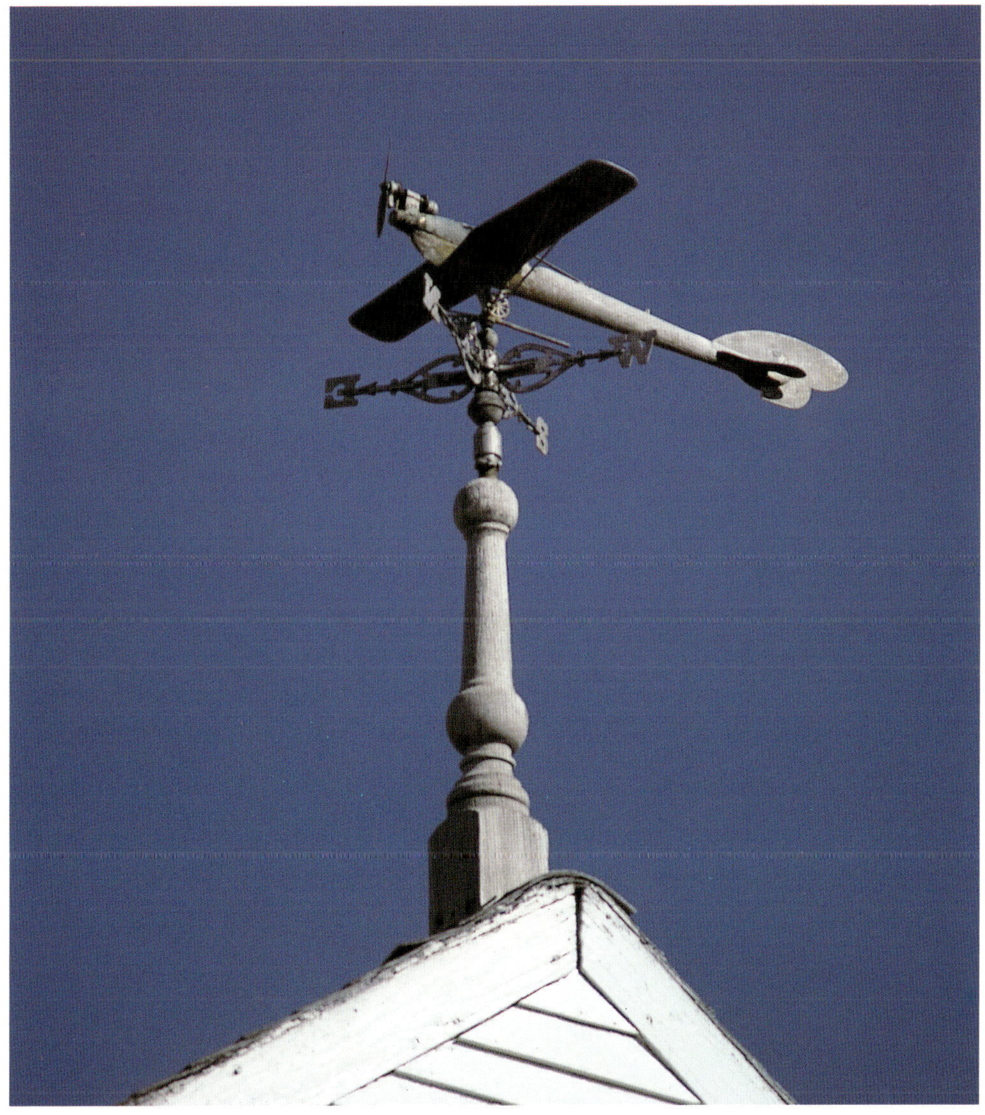

A hammered-copper log driver made by Skowhegan craftsman Barry Norling was placed on a Skowhegan bank in 1984. For years, the Kennebec River, which runs through Skowhegan, was used for driving logs to area paper mills from the upper Kennebec River Valley. The logger's face conveys strength and determination.

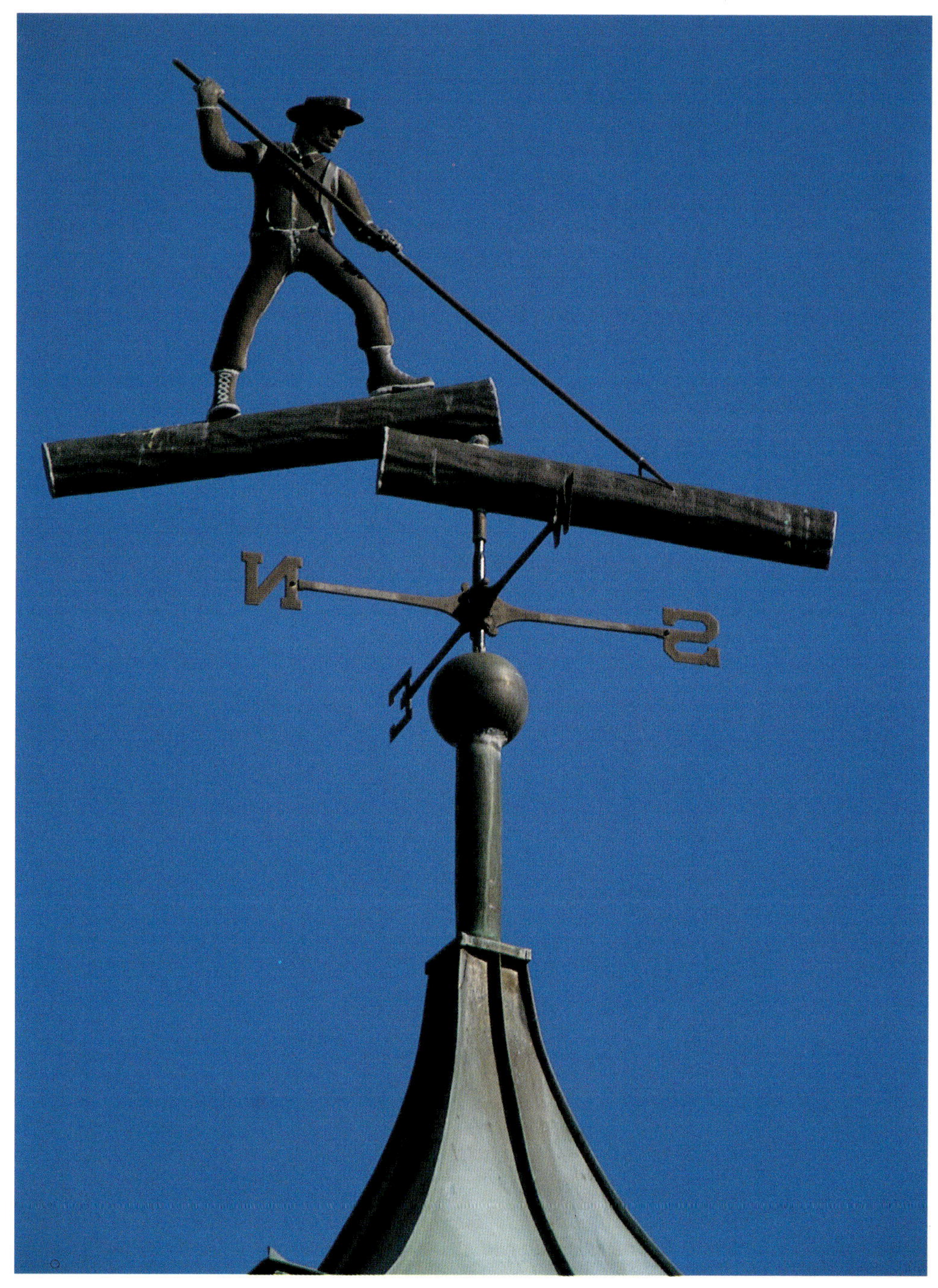

It took a look through a telephoto lens to show show the details of this small flowing figure. it appears to be a night watchman, ringing a bell with his right hand and holding a lantern in his left. The folds on the cloak and mantle are sweeping the form along.

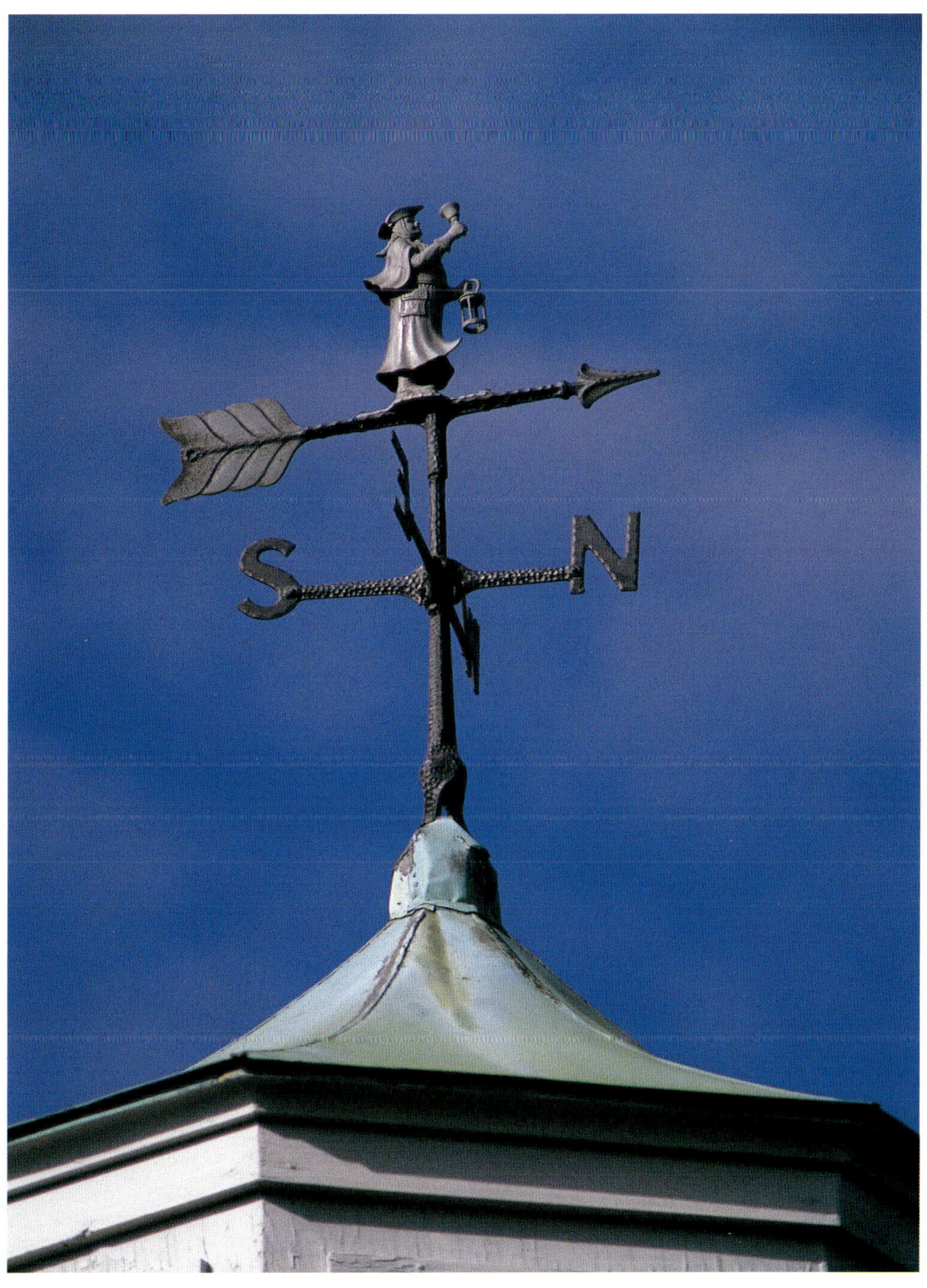

The lady at her loom makes a fascinating silhouette. This detailed cut-out dates from 1937, and pays tribute to Maine's once thriving textile industry. Since the time when this photo was taken, the vane has been gilded.

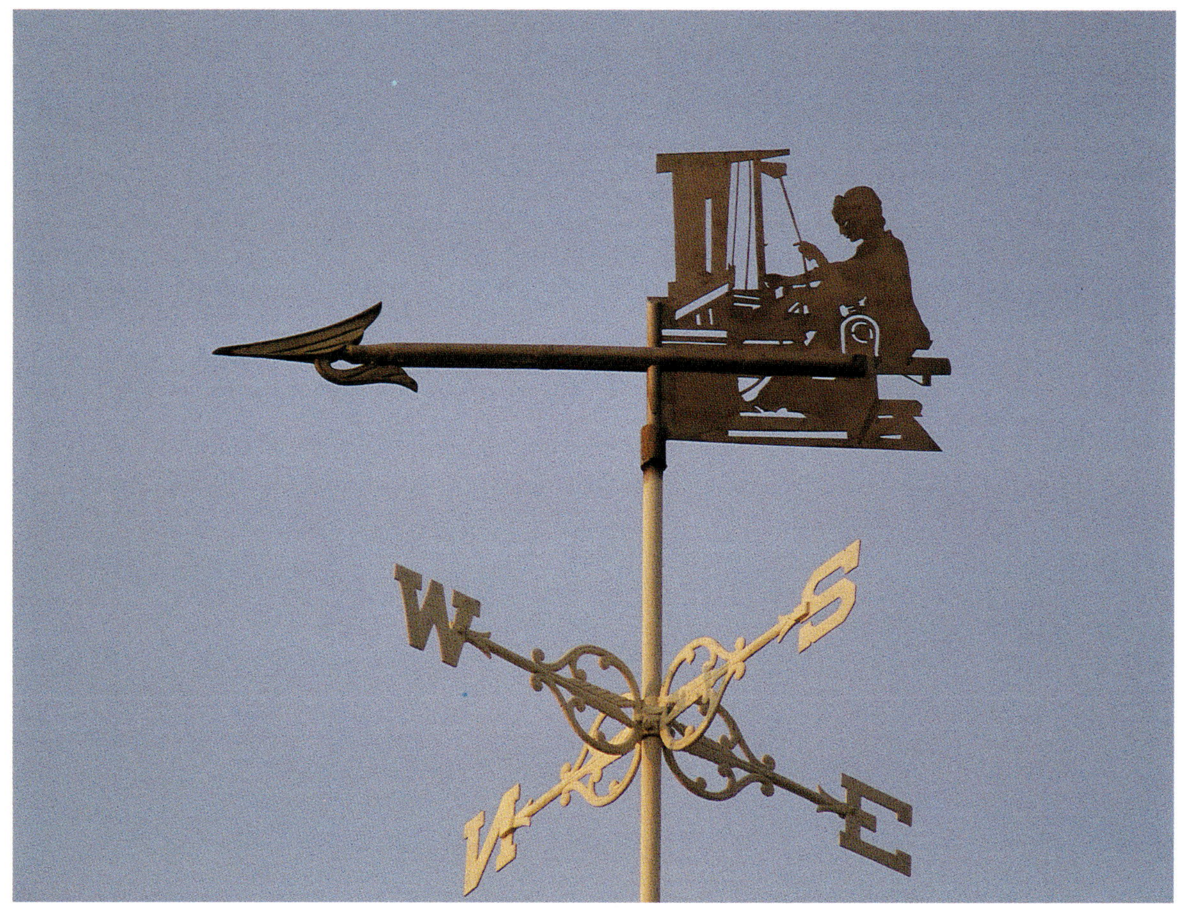

The gleaming eyes staring out of the total blackness of the chimney sweep make this vane an arresting sight. The cardinals have a nice circular design. As one might suspect, this vane tops the home of a professional chimney sweep.

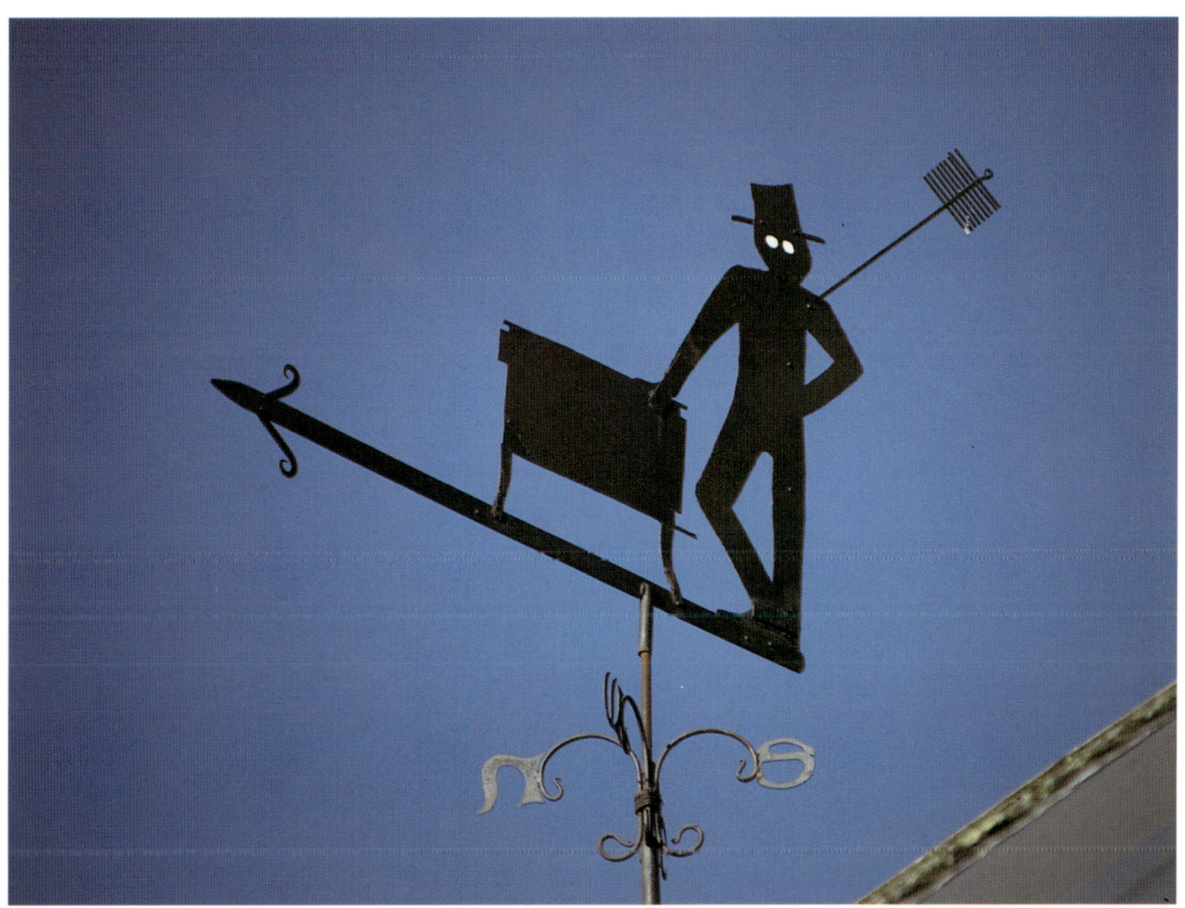

It should come as no surprise that this new copper vane belongs to cross-country skiing enthusiasts, who brought it to Maine from Cape Cod.

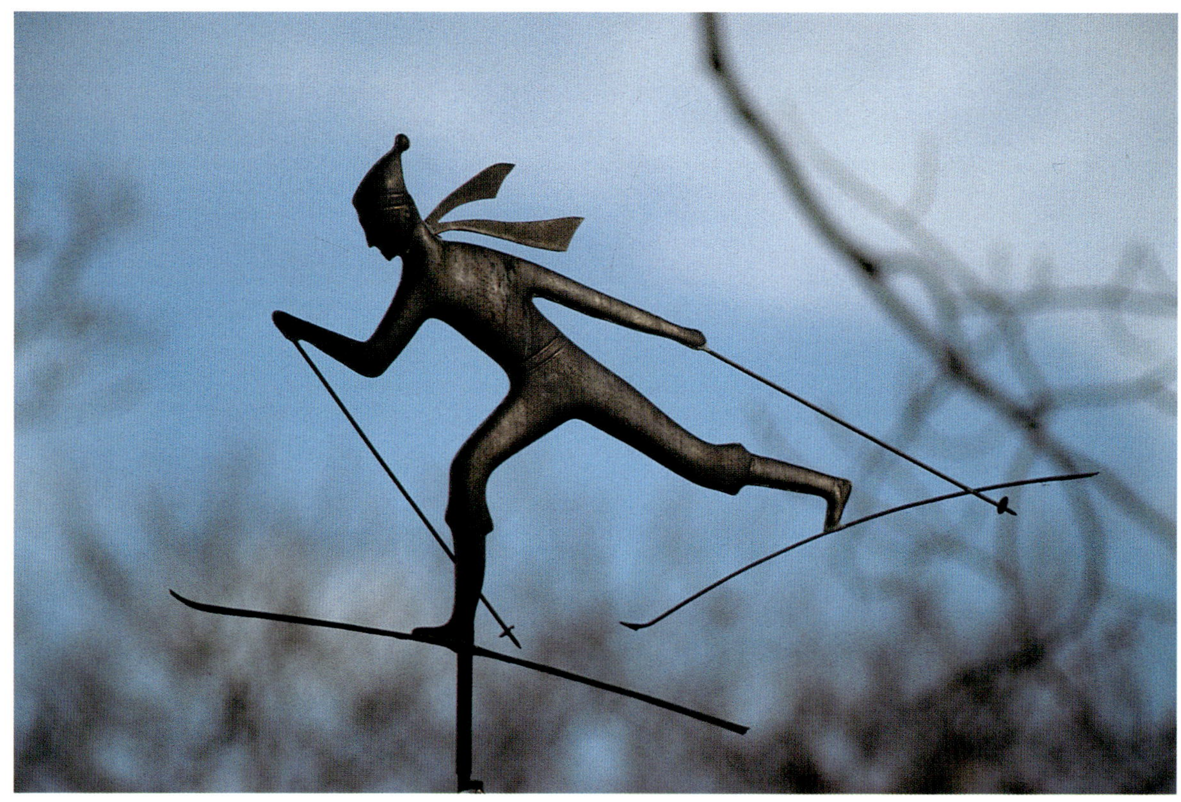

Bibliography

Benes, Peter. *New England Meeting House and Church: 1630–1850.* Boston University and The Currier Gallery of Art: 1979.

Bishop, Robert. *A Gallery of American Weathervanes and Whirligigs.* New York: E.P. Dutton & Co., 1981.

Jones, Herbert G. *Maine Memories.* Portland, Maine: Harmon Publishing Co., 1940.

Kaye, Myrna. *Yankee Weathervanes.* New York: E.P. Dutton & Co., 1975.

Miller, Steve. *The Art of the Weathervane.* Exton, Pennsylvania: Schiffer Publishing Ltd., 1984.

Museums Displaying Weather Vanes

Abby Aldrich Rockefeller Folk Art Center, Williamsburg, Virginia
American Folk Art Gallery, New York, New York
Concord Antiquarian Society, Concord, Massachusetts
The Currier Gallery of Art, Manchester, New Hampshire
George E. Schoellhopf Gallery, New York, New York
Greenfield Village and the Henry Ford Museum, Dearborn, Michigan
The Henry Francis duPont Winterthur Museum, Winterthur, Delaware
Historical Society of Pennsylvania, Philadelphia, Pennsylvania
Marna Anderson Gallery, New York, New York
Mingei International, San Diego, California
Museum of American Folk Art, New York, New York
Museum of Fine Arts, Boston, Massachusetts
Museum of International Folk Art, Santa Fe, New Mexico
Museum of the New York State Historical Association, Cooperstown, New York
Nantucket Historical Association, Nantucket, Massachusetts
New Bedford Whaling Museum, New Bedford, Massachusetts
The Newark Museum, Newark, New Jersey
Shelburne Museum, Shelburne, Vermont
Wenham Historical Museum, Wenham, Massachusetts
William A. Farnsworth Museum and Art Gallery, Rockland, Maine